Frederick Ryland

Ethics: an introductory manual for the use of university students

Frederick Ryland

Ethics: an introductory manual for the use of university students

ISBN/EAN: 9783337215095

Printed in Europe, USA, Canada, Australia, Japan

Cover: Foto ©Lupo / pixelio.de

More available books at **www.hansebooks.com**

ETHICS:

AN INTRODUCTORY MANUAL FOR THE USE OF UNIVERSITY STUDENTS.

BY

F. RYLAND, M.A.,

AUTHOR OF "A HANDBOOK OF PSYCHOLOGY," "CHRONOLOGICAL OUTLINES OF ENGLISH LITERATURE," ETC.

LONDON:
GEORGE BELL & SONS, YORK ST., COVENT GARDEN.
NEW YORK: 112, FOURTH AVENUE.
1893.

CHISWICK PRESS:—CHARLES WHITTINGHAM AND CO., TOOKS COURT,
CHANCERY LANE.

PREFACE.

THE object of the following pages is to give a sketch of ethical theory designed in the main on the customary English lines as laid down in the regulations of the University of London. At the same time I have not bound myself slavishly to follow those lines, but have introduced discussions on the speculations of the so-called Evolutionary school of Mr. Spencer and Mr. Leslie Stephen, and the Oxford neo-Hegelian school founded by the late T. H. Green. This course, though adding somewhat to the difficulty of the book, seems justifiable by the additional interest given to the subject. I have also ventured to suggest a revival of a more æsthetic attitude in dealing with Ethics; something more akin, as I take it, to that assumed by the Greek thinkers, from whom the science of conduct takes its origin.

In chapter i. I discuss the general scope and method of the science; in chapters ii. and iii. the principal concepts of the science are dealt with, viz., Good and Right and their dependent categories. In chapters iv. and v. the various Hedonistic and anti-Hedonistic theories are explained and criticised.

Chapter vi. is devoted to a consideration of some of the chief psychological questions involved in Ethics. In chapter vii. various classifications of the excellences of conduct are discussed. Chapter viii. is mainly devoted to the relation between Ethics, Theology, and Law. Chapter ix. gives a short historical account of the chief English moralists. In the Appendix will be found full directions as to further and wider reading, and the questions set in the subject at the London B.A. examination during the last ten years.

A few pages have been taken almost verbatim from the second part of my " Handbook of Psychology and Ethics."

It only remains for me to thank my friend Mr. Joseph Jacobs for reading through the proofs and making several suggestions which will add to the practical value of the book.

PUTNEY,
December, 1892.

CONTENTS.

CHAPTER I.
Scope and Method.

	PAGE
§ 1. The Subject of the Ethical Judgment	1
2. The Predicate of the Ethical Judgment	5
3. Ethical Judgments—Reasoning	7
4. The Science of Ethics	13
5. Progress in Ethics	15
6. Classification of Ethical Theories	16
7. Evolutionary Ethics	19

CHAPTER II.
Good, Happiness, Perfection.

§ 1. The Good	21
2. Fame; Wisdom	24
3. Happiness	25
4. Pleasure	28
5. Excellence or Perfection	33
6. The Summum Bonum	37
7. Humanity	41
8. God	42
9. Good as essentially Relative	43

CHAPTER III.
Right, Obligation, Duty.

§ 1. Right	46
2. The Standard of Right	48

CONTENTS.

	PAGE
§ 3. Rights	50
4. Jus Naturale	51
5. Obligation	53
6. Duty	57
7. Virtue	62
8. Merit	64
9. Responsibility	65

CHAPTER IV.
HEDONISTIC THEORIES.

§ 1. The Hedonistic Calculus	68
2. The Commensurability of Pleasures	70
3. Uncertainty of our Hedonic Judgments	73
4. Failure of Arithmetical Hedonism	75
5. Egoism and Altruism	76
6. Utilitarianism	79
7. The Proof of Utilitarianism	83
8. Objections to Utilitarianism with regard to Distribution	88
9. The Vagueness of Utilitarianism	92
10. Evolutionary Hedonism	95

CHAPTER V.
INTUITIONIST THEORIES.

§ 1. The word Intuition	100
2. Relation between Intuitionism and Hedonism	102
3. Intuitionism	103
4. Dogmatic Intuitionism	105
5. Philosophic Intuitionism	109
6. Objections to Intuitionism	114
7. Other so-called Intuitionist Theories	117
8. Life according to Nature	119
9. Perfectionism	122
10. The Æsthetic View	124
11. Objections to the Æsthetic View	128

CHAPTER VI.

THE PSYCHOLOGY OF ETHICS.

	PAGE
§ 1. Connection between Psychology and Ethics	133
2. The Moral Faculty	135
3. Moral Sense	137
4. Moral Reason	139
5. Moral Emotions	144
6. Conscience	147
7. Pleasure and Desire	150
8. Motive and Intention	153
9. Freedom of the Will	155
10. Habit	159
11. Is Wrong-doing Involuntary?	161

CHAPTER VII.

THE CLASSIFICATION OF MORAL EXCELLENCES.

§ 1. The Consistency of Moral Excellences	165
2. Classification adopted by Early Moralists	165
3. Duties to Self and to our Neighbour	169
4. Prudence	173
5. Courage	175
6. Temperance	175
7. Justice	176

CHAPTER VIII.

ETHICS IN RELATION TO THEOLOGY AND LAW.

§ 1. Ethics and Theology	179
2. Morality and Law	181
3. Obedience to Law	183
4. Casuistry	185

CHAPTER IX.

BRIEF SKETCH OF ENGLISH ETHICAL THEORIES.

	PAGE
§ 1. Hobbes and his Opponents	188
2. Shaftesbury and Butler	190
3. Hutcheson, Hume, and Smith	193
4. Paley, Bentham, and Mill	195
5. Tabular View of English Ethical Theories up to Mill	198

APPENDICES.

A. Books Recommended	199
B. Questions for London University B.A. Pass Papers, 1883-1892	212
INDEX	217

ETHICS.

CHAPTER I.

SCOPE AND METHOD.

§ 1. The Subject of the Ethical Judgment.

We are constantly passing judgments on the actions of ourselves and of others. We describe some acts as good, some as bad, and others again, perhaps, as indifferent. And in the same way we pass judgment on connected series of acts deliberately pursued, on what is called " conduct." Reflection shows that it is really as forming part of such a series of motives, judgments and acts, that we consider a given act as good, bad, or indifferent. An isolated act, regarded in the abstract and without reference to the acts preceding it, the motives which prompt it and the effects produced by it, is not properly the subject of an ethical judgment. Thus, suppose A inserts a knife into B, and thereby causes his death. Whether A's conduct is regarded as praiseworthy or the reverse depends on whether A is prompted by revenge or by desire to alleviate suffering, whether A is a properly qualified surgeon or an ignorant quack, whether the circumstances in which B is placed warrant a dangerous operation or forbid it.

Primarily then we pass ethical judgments on conduct. This excludes purely automatic acts, except in so far as previous voluntary acts have rendered them possible, likely, or inevitable.[1] Those habitual acts, however, which are still conscious and in a sense voluntary, are included. All voluntary and habitual acts, linked together by common purposes consciously formulated, are collectively called conduct.

We have seen that the motive with which an act is undertaken, as well as the end at which it aims, helps to determine our opinion of it. These purely psychological facts take their place in our conception of conduct, but they are so important that some moralists lay down that they are the really determining features.

Given a right end and a right motive the act is good; at any rate, unless end and motive are right the act is not in a moral sense really excellent. If A saves B's life by an act intended to destroy it, or even as an unintended consequence of an act directed to another end, we do not count it a meritorious act on the part of A.

That rightness of motive is alone necessary seems to be the general opinion among the accredited teachers of conduct. Cardinal Newman, for instance, tells us that it is our duty to follow conscience even if conscience bids us reject the claims of the Catholic Church; the materially or objectively good act of

---

[1] See below, chap. iii. § 9.

accepting the Faith becomes formally or subjectively wrong if it is done in opposition to our conscience. And Kant and Hutcheson among philosophers agree that as long as the motive is right the act is virtuous.

Common sense, however, is hardly satisfied with this extreme position. The motives of a Torquemada or a Robespierre may be as pure as those of a St. Francis of Assisi or a Gordon, but the world will not consider them as equally good men. We should not regard a homicidal pessimist, who sought under the influence of the sincerest philanthropy to destroy human life by some wholesale application of scientific means, as a good man. Something else is necessary unless our ethical theory is to bring us into direct antagonism with the moral judgments of the majority of civilized men. We must refrain from assuming that ethical judgments have for their proper subject merely motive or intention.

It may be urged, however, that *character* or *disposition* is the proper subject of ethical judgment. But unless carefully explained this throws us back on the view we have just been discussing. As usually applied, the term character means the permanent tendency to particular kinds of conduct, the dominant modes of volition. It is partly inherited and partly acquired. A good character is one which is constituted by the " possession of certain acquired tendencies or habitudes which we call virtues." The relation between character and conduct is thus very close. " Think of a man's conduct in relation to the mental conditions from which it proceeds and you think of his character; think of his character as it produces results beyond these sentiments themselves and you have conduct."[1] This comes again to motive, although a new element is added, namely, the strength of will, the constancy with which the will remains true to a motive and the degree of completeness with which it obliges action to correspond with motive.

As we have rejected the view that makes goodness or badness of motive the sufficient criterion, we are led back to conduct as the proper subject of moral judgment. By conduct we mean the action of a human being regarded as forming a connected series, in agreement with the permanent dictates of his intellect and feelings. The acts of the hypnotic patient or of the idiot are not conduct; but the acts of the madman in so far as under the control of his own mind, however disturbed and disorganized that mind may be, may be fairly described as conduct, and they are therefore in some degree open to the application of ethical judgments. Purely reflex acts form no part of conduct; but acts which, although normally unconscious or involuntary, may under suitable conditions (subject to our control) be rendered voluntary, are included in it. Thus psychological considerations are involved in the notion of conduct. But they are not the sole or chief thing to be considered. And although we have to take them into account, we shall have to define good

[1] Alexander, "Moral Order and Progress," p. 49. Cf. Sully, "Outlines of Psychology," p. 439 *seq*.

motive and character by reference to good conduct and not *vice versâ*.

Ethics then is the science of conduct. It seeks to ascertain what conduct is good or right, and what bad or wrong. It does not deal with the nature of the isolated act, or with the motive or intention alone, or with the character of the agent alone. It deals with acts as forming part of a connected series and takes into account the psychological causes and effects of those acts.

§ 2. The Predicate of the Ethical Judgment.

We find ourselves and others constantly making assertions about acts or series of acts, about motives or intentions, and about characters. We say that such an act, or impulse, or person, is brave, prudent, just: thereby tacitly implying that we can form an idea of bravery, prudence, or justice, and that we can form classes of acts, impulses, or persons possessing in common the attributes.

This is the first stage of the ethical judgment. The science of ethics took its rise in the attempt made by Socrates to isolate and define the common element which was to be found in all brave acts, all prudent acts, all just acts. And a great deal of the most useful part of ethics must consist in thus classifying and analysing our primary moral predicates. Unfortunately, however, modern writers on ethics have concerned themselves but little with this branch of their subject.

Their neglect is due partly to the revolt against casuistry, that is, the systematic consideration of difficult moral cases, because it is chiefly in the discussion of such limiting cases that we get accurate knowledge as to what we mean by the predicate whose applicability is called in question. It is partly due to the mainly psychological turn which English philosophy has always tended to take; which substitutes an investigation into the origin of an idea for a consideration of its validity.

And again, it is partly due to a desire to carry on ethical discussion in the region of the higher ethical categories, for it has usually seemed more hopeful to the philosopher to consider the good and the right at large, than to consider more concrete cases, just as the earlier biologists were always trying to analyse life in general, and the earlier psychologists preferred to start from the notion of the Ego, although this method of approaching the problems has of late fallen into disrepute.

The next step is to see what common element brave acts and prudent acts and just acts, motives or characters, all exhibit. But we must remember that they may be considered from the psychological or the æsthetic point of view as well as the ethical. The psychologist is interested in the general mental conditions and results of a brave act; the poet or artist is interested in the beauty of it. The ethical thinker, although not indifferent to either, is concerned with another aspect of the brave act. He judges it to be *good* and *right*. What is the meaning of these terms which form the predicates of what may be called the secondary ethical judgments? What exactly is implied in these assertions? This is the part of ethics which has received most attention. It is certainly less practical, and it does not seem more easy, than the more concrete part; but it has proved more interesting.

Besides the terms *good* and *right*, there are a few others which may be resolved into them, or at any rate can be connected with them, such as *obligatory, meritorious, virtuous,* etc. The duty of the ethical thinker is obviously to examine (1) what is meant by each of these terms—what is its connotation? And (2) To what conduct each of these terms can be properly applied—what is its denotation? Of these two questions the former has received much more attention than the latter. Chapters ii.-vi. of this book will be devoted to it, while chapter vii. will deal with the second question.

In the typical ethical judgment, then, the subject will be conduct—or act, motive or character in subordination to conduct; the predicate will be some primary term, such as brave or just, or some wider term, such as good or right.

§ 3. Ethical Judgments—Reasoning.

The greater part of ethical judgments are what logicians call synthetic or ampliative; that is, they assert of the subject some attribute which is not implied by the subject itself. There are of course analytic judgments, as there are in other sciences, declaring the meaning of terms; but the ultimate premises do not belong to this class of proposition. If we say that "the greatest happiness of the greatest number is a right end of action," our assertion is strictly synthetic. The question arises, is it synthetic *à posteriori*, like those of the positive sciences, that is, gained by observation and induction; or is it synthetic *à priori*, like the ultimate axioms of mathematics, that is, obtained by some process of direct inspection?

By what process do we come to form correct ethical judgments? In other words, what is the logical method of ethics?

At first sight our moral judgments appear to have a very immediate character. They seem to record the result of a mere process of perception. When we say "this act is right," still more when we say "that act is wrong," the judgment seems to be almost as direct as when we say "this object is hot." Such judgments are usually regarded as the normal deliverances of conscience, which is supposed to speak instantaneously, and in normal cases unerringly. The child is taught to trust these quasi-perceptions without question; and the popular dislike of casuistry and scientific ethics is due to the belief that the usual effect of reasoning about questions of right and wrong is to obscure the naturally clear deliverances of what is called the moral sense. If this view be correct ethics must be a purely inductive science. Its primary object will be to collect, record, and systematize the moral precepts of normal individuals, and to note and explain the real or apparent deviations in those of abnormal individuals. General propositions, analogous to the laws of other inductive sciences, will no doubt be discovered, but they will have no practical importance. We do not need the generalization of optics to tell us more readily or certainly what things are luminous, nor will general ethical truths enable us more easily to discover what conduct is right. Ethical writers accustomed to their own critical point of view do not seem to realize how widely this view (which, as Professor Sidgwick says, is at once "ultra-intuitional" and "ultra-empirical"), is held by ordinary persons. It is the current ethical philosophy, not only of the nursery and the pulpit, but of the average plain man. Yet the ground on which it rests is in the highest degree uncertain. Our moral percepts or quasi-percepts are often vague, indefinite, and, worse still, conflicting. Unlike the percepts of the senses, they do not bear strict examination. The more I attend to a sense-percept, so long as the organ does not become fatigued, the clearer it becomes. By repeating the observation under varying conditions I become more and more sure. But the immediate and unreasoned utterances of conscience do not normally become more definite by concentrating attention on them. Nor do we find anything like a general agreement in these apparent percepts, such as we find in the percepts of the senses. The ethical intuitions of the vast majority of the human race are avowedly erroneous, or at least extremely imperfect. It is only those of the civilized and Christianized races that have any claim to be regarded as correct. Even among these there is great want of unanimity. Let us ask in a general company the question whether it is right to use the formula "not at home" in some specified set of conditions where it is not literally true, and we shall find that the replies are various, and that they do not rest for the most part on unambiguous intuitions, but palpably depend on a process of reasoning.

As a matter of fact, this "perceptional intuitionism" is not the teaching of any school of thinkers. Systematic theologians reject it as well as philosophers. Certain general propositions are held to be of higher certainty than the particular quasi-percepts of conscience, and in order to know the moral quality of an act, we have to bring it under one or more of these universals. We feel the need of a deductive process, and our practical syllogism takes some such form as this :

"To assist others in trouble is right (or obligatory).

"This is such an act of assistance.

"Therefore, this is right (or obligatory)."

The truth of the minor premise may sometimes be so readily recognized, that the process may take the form of a percept. But this is seldom the case. Reflection generally discloses that the minor premise is itself guaranteed by a further process of reasoning, though this is seldom difficult to construct. The more onerous task is to determine how the major premise is guaranteed.

Obviously deduction alone cannot justify it. We must come at last to some moral judgment which cannot be inferred from any higher one. The ultimate ethical major premise, or premises, must be due either to induction or to intuition.

Induction may take as its starting point definite objective facts, which are capable of proof, *e.g.*, the conduciveness of certain acts to pleasure. But we cannot in this way prove more than that such acts do conduce to pleasure; we cannot show that they *ought* to be performed, or that they are ethically right. We could only prove their obligation or rightness by starting from perception of obligation or rightness in the individual cases. Such perceptions do not exist, for moral quality is not a fact of perception; it has no relation to space and time.

We may, however, start not from facts of perception, but from the moral opinions of men. By collecting and generalizing these we may arrive at moral laws, which will represent the normal opinions of ourselves and others as to what is morally good or the reverse, in the same way as the principles of art represent the normal opinions as to what is beautiful. This is much the same kind of induction as that which

Aristotle tells us Socrates applied to ethics. It rests wholly on facts of feeling, which cannot be justified or criticized. Feeling cannot test its own validity. And feelings vary. It is only by arbitrarily excluding the savage and the man of earlier civilizations that we can get any approach to uniformity of moral feeling. Besides, there is much less uniformity in our own moral approbation and disapprobation than is commonly supposed. Theologians and philosophers differ between themselves, as well as the civilized man from the savage. Women approve and disapprove differently from men. If we ask what virtue they estimate most highly, to which they would postpone all others, the woman and the man, the philosopher and the hero, the philanthropist and the theologian, will give different replies.

It seems then a somewhat hopeless task to base our ethics on inductive inferences from the facts of moral feeling, if we regard ethics as a science of the same kind as the positive sciences, which give us definite conclusions resting on a more or less certain basis of axioms or observations, as the case may be. If, however, we are willing to regard it as parallel rather to æsthetics than to these, we may well be contented with the basis thus described. But like æsthetics we shall expect ethics to give us no absolute principles, only to tell us what normally meets with the approval of cultivated moral perception, and to explain why. We shall have to come back to the attitude of Aristotle, who lays down that abstract accuracy cannot be expected in ethics, the subject matter of which does not permit of demonstrative certainty. Although by induction we cannot prove that any end, say pleasure, ought to be the end of conduct, we can prove that most wise men think it so, and we must be content with this result. We shall have to allow that *desirable* means merely what is desired by those whose opinions we value most; and we shall have to take a purely relative view of the meaning of *obligation* and of *right*.

The alternative to induction as the guarantee of our ultimate major premises must be intuition. If these premises are not obtained by generalization from particular facts or particular judgments, they must be recognized as true immediately on mere inspection, like the axioms of mathematics. Their validity must be guaranteed in the act of understanding them. Such is the theory of those philosophers who are called Intuitionists or Intuitionalists. It makes the science of ethics essentially deductive, and assimilates it in some degree to the science of geometry.

It will be noted that in this view we must be prepared to find our theoretical conclusions sometimes at variance with received moral judgments. Induction may serve as a check, but it is not valid against careful deductive conclusions from moral axioms.

§ 4. The Science of Ethics.

Science examines its data and proves their reality and validity; it classifies them, arranging them so that they can be handled most conveniently; and it draws from them conclusions either more general, by induction, or more special, by deduction.

So in ethics, we find a portion of the science devoted to showing the nature of moral judgments, what their objectivity and validity really means. This part of the science is largely psychological, because the nature and validity of the judgments depend to some extent on the mental processes on which they rest. Questions as to the character of the moral faculty are almost necessarily implied. We deal with such terms as Conscience, Moral Reason, Moral Intuition, etc.

These deliverances of our moral faculties, percepts, concepts, judgments, and emotions, are brought under each other in proper subordination. Classes and subclasses of moral predicates are formed, and the relations of these categories to each other are considered. We have to determine what is meant by brave and just, good and right, obligation and merit, end and means, standard and sanction, real and ideal.

We must then seek to extend the classification beyond the points usually recognized — to bring special cases under general laws, to show that concepts apply to facts which have not been considered in connection with them. The bindingness of certain kinds of conduct, hitherto regarded as praiseworthy and not as obligatory, the incompatibility of ideals usually treated as practically equivalent, such inferences as these will be found in works on ethics.

In these respects the science of ethics will necessarily be like other sciences. But its special character lies in the admission of the ideal element. A merely positive ethics which does no more than recognize that certain rules are usually observed, and does not regard them as in any sense binding, is no ethics at all, but a branch of anthropology or sociology. There is need for an ideal element; such or such a rule ought to be observed, such or such an excellence ought to be aimed at, is implied in the terms right or good. The ideal is not necessarily given by any special faculty; it may be supplied by imagination, which carries on and develops the result of induction or experience. In this way ethics resembles jurisprudence, æsthetics, and other practical sciences. It does not merely describe what is, but seeks to describe what ought to be.

§ 5. Progress in Ethics.

It is usually acknowledged that there is progress in ethics. This may mean (1) that men conform better to rules they have always recognized but not always obeyed, or (2) that they gradually come to recognize a new standard of conduct as binding on them. Both forms of improvement usually go together; to raise the standard commonly implies greater efforts to conform to it; and a higher level of practice usually involves wider and nobler views of what is incumbent on us.

At the same time, if standards change, we see that

our standard may become obsolete. What then is the relation of the higher standard to the lower? Is it mere contradiction? There is affirmation as well as denial. Cases which were previously not recognized as coming under some given moral rule are brought under it, as the subject matter is better understood, as imagination enables us to picture the conditions of such cases, and as sympathy widens. Thus women and negroes have in different ways and at different times been brought within the scope of moral relations. In earlier times they were ill-treated simply because even good men did not realize that they could rationally be regarded in the same way as males, and as white people, respectively.

The advance to a new position does not imply the absolute denial of the old one, but its inclusion in a wider formula which will embrace both. At the same time during the progress of the revolution there is often partial forgetfulness of what has already been learnt. When the movement is completed it will usually be found that what was valuable in the original position has been preserved as well as what is valuable in the new.

§ 6. Classification of Ethical Theories.

For the convenience of the reader it is worth while to anticipate a little and give here a rough classification of the chief ethical theories.[1] We may hold that a certain action is incumbent on us because it is neces-

[1] See Dr. Sidgwick's "Methods of Ethics," bk. i., chap. i.

sary to a certain end that we are aiming at; or we may hold that the action is incumbent on us, not because it conduces to any end, but in itself, and without reference to its consequences. A theory of Ethics that regards certain rules as absolutely obligatory, without explicit reference to their ultimate consequences, is called an *independent* system of Ethics. A theory that makes the rightness of actions depend on their conduciveness to some assumed end is called a *dependent* or *relative* system of Ethics.

Reflection seems to show that there are only two things which men regard as intrinsically reasonable ends of conduct, viz.: (i) Perfection or excellence, and (ii) Happiness. Either of these ultimate ends, Perfection and Happiness, may be sought—(*a*) for oneself alone, or (*b*) for all. We thus get five main possible views of Ethics:—

I. Independent, or Intuitive

II. Dependent, taking as an end
- 1. Perfection
  - (*a*) of oneself
  - (*b*) of all
- 2. Happiness
  - (*a*) of oneself
  - (*b*) of all

The four dependent theories may be respectively called Egoistic and Universalistic Perfectionism, and Egoistic and Universalistic Hedonism.[1] Practically,

[1] Hedonism means a system of Ethics that takes Pleasure (ἡδονή) as the ultimate end of all truly rational action. We may add here, that a theory of absolute Altruism, or regard *only* for others, is perhaps ideally possible.

however, the moralists, who take Perfection or Excellence as the rational end of conduct, consider Virtue as by far the most important element in the Excellence aimed at, and Virtue they usually assume to mean " the observance of certain rules of duty intuitively known." Hence, to a large extent, the first dependent method coincides with the independent or intuitive method. On the other hand, if the hedonistic view of Virtue be taken by a Perfectionist, his theory of conduct will hardly differ from those pure Hedonists who explicitly set happiness or pleasure as their ultimate end. Thus we reduce the methods to three:—(1) *Intuitionism*, in which the standard or criterion of conduct is conformity to absolute rules of duty intuitively known; (2) *Egoistic Hedonism*, the theory which takes as the standard of conduct conduciveness to the happiness of I-myself; (3) *Universalistic Hedonism*, which takes as its standard conduciveness to the happiness of all. It is this third method that is properly called Utilitarianism, using the word in its historical meaning, to denote the moral philosophy of Bentham and Mill.

Many Perfectionists, however, object to this identification of their view with Intuitionism. The content which is given to the idea of good is not due, they say, to any special process of intuition, but to the ordinary intellectual activities. But this objection seems to arise from a mistake as to the true meaning of intuition, which is the mere antithesis of inference. It does not imply the existence of any particular faculty of moral perception as apart from the other faculties, something transcending ordinary experience, infallible and quasi-miraculous.[1]

§ 7. Evolutionary Ethics.

Perfectionism is not the only ethical theory which it is difficult to bring under our scheme. Some recent writers practically make Ethics a part of Sociology. The object of the science, they hold, is to systematically determine the proper activities of an individual as a unit in the organic whole we call society. They shift the point of view from the individual to the whole, of which he is a part. They wish to discover the conduct which most tends to the preservation or well-being of society; and to discover it by considering the conditions under which society has been developed. That is, "they attempt to deduce moral rules from biological or sociological laws. This latter procedure," adds Dr. Sidgwick, with some *naïveté*, " is sometimes called ' establishing morality on a scientific basis.' "[2] That conduct is right which tends to the welfare of society, in other words, which tends to the greater organic health of society. The progressive adaptation of society to its changing environment is possible only by the gradually improving adjustment of activities within it. The change which we call "progress" is one which renders society more capable of continuance by increasing its vitality. Evolutionists assume that this series of changes is

---

[1] See below, chap. v., § 1.
[2] " History of Ethics," p. 246 (2nd edit.).

itself desirable; that society ought to exist and ought therefore to improve. The proposition that social progress, from an indefinite, incoherent homogeneity towards a definite coherent heterogeneity, is itself desirable (whether from the point of view of the race or of the individual) cannot easily be proved. It is conceivable that greater progress measured in this way might involve the gradual disappearance of consciousness, or the increasing prevalence of pain, as some pessimists have believed. By the use of biological metaphors we cannot escape from the need of ethically justifying the *terminus ad quem* supposed to be scientifically predicted. Is the welfare of society a desirable end for me, even if it means suffering to me or to human beings generally?

Most of the evolutionary school, for instance Mr. Spencer and Mr. Leslie Stephen, lay down that, broadly speaking, social progress necessarily involves greater pleasure to the individual. Mr. Spencer, indeed, confesses that otherwise it would not be desirable. This admission, and the assertion of the pre-established harmony between social welfare and individual happiness enable us to class Mr. Spencer and his school as Hedonists.[1]

[1] See below, chap. iv., § 10.

CHAPTER II.

GOOD, HAPPINESS, PERFECTION.

§ 1. The Good.

THE ultimate meaning of Good seems to be what satisfies desire.[1] We regard the capacity for satisfying desire as an objective attribute of the thing. The judgment, "this is good," is the intellectual correlative of the fact of desire.

It is the business of ethics to settle what is truly desirable; the discussion of what is desired belongs to psychology. Speaking broadly, the two are not necessarily connected. It is conceivable that while psychology might show that men always desire pleasure, ethics might prove that pleasure is never really desirable. The main work of the Greek thinkers who laid the foundation of ethics was to differentiate from each other the two things; and in the later Greek and in the Latin moralists we get the distinction in the form of the antithesis between interest and duty. The desirable is the desired looked at *sub specie juris*, what we are morally bound to desire; and thus in

---

[1] Spinoza, "Ethics," Part III., Prop. ix. and xxxix.

modern ethics the idea of good is often regarded as secondary to that of ought, or right. On this view we must know what ought means, in order to know what good means.[1]

Nearly all good things turn out on reflection to be good only as means to something else, to be only relative goods. They are conditional, in that they presuppose the goodness of the end to which they are means. Money is good as a means to happiness, and careful bookkeeping as a means to making money. We seem, then, bound to assume that there are some things which are good in themselves. It is commonly assumed that there can be only one *summum bonum*, and that all other goods can only justify themselves by showing that they are means to this. Still, *primâ facie*, there are several ends which lay claim to finality, and while in practice there is pretty general agreement, at any rate verbal agreement, as to the relative importance of the subordinate goods, there is considerable speculative difficulty in settling the relations of those which have claims to the position of *summum genus*. We all agree that money is good simply as a means; we most of us agree that health is good simply as a means. When we ask "a means to what?" uncertainty begins.

---

[1] Moral good is sometimes distinguished from natural good, that is, from all other goods. The antithesis is not absolute, since good conduct is defined by many schools of thinkers as that conduct which secures the supreme good; by hedonists (*e.g.*) as that conduct which secures pleasure.

Aristotle ("Nic. Eth.," I. vii.) seems to regard it as a test of the *summum bonum* that it shall never be chosen as a means, but always as an end. This, however, is not necessary. Pleasure may be, as the hedonists say, the ultimate end, and moral excellence only valuable as a means to pleasure; nevertheless a consistent hedonist may desire to be pleased with his dinner in order that he may be good-tempered and benevolent on a critical occasion, while he justifies the benevolence on account of its hedonic result to himself and others.

We may assume that the highest good we are in search of will be a good attainable by man. By a good, even when used in its most absolute sense, we mean good for man. Indeed, when we say "God is good," we either use the term good as equivalent to morally excellent, or we imply that God is an object of enjoyment.[1] We shall not hold with Plato that the good is out of relation to ourselves and human nature in general, that it is something which exists in and for itself in a world of ideas. Nor, on the other hand, will it be purely relative, merely what each man, in whatever stage of moral development, thinks good. Rather it will be what the ideally wise man ($\dot{o}\ \phi\rho\acute{o}\nu\iota\mu o\varsigma$) judges good.

The following appear to be the goods which have been regarded by men as absolute and final: Fame,

---

[1] St. Anselm, "Monologium," cap. i. Cf. Dante, "Paradiso," xxvi. This view has only an antiquarian interest.

Wisdom, Happiness, Pleasure, Perfection, Humanity, God.

§ 2. Fame; Wisdom.

Fame.—Contemporary fame or honour may be always regarded as a means to happiness or pleasure. Even posthumous fame may be represented as deriving its desirability from the pleasure which the anticipatory contemplation of it gives to the individual himself. Although a limited number of men have apparently regarded posthumous fame, or even disgraceful notoriety, as an absolute end for which they have sacrificed happiness, excellence, and perhaps even the consciousness of present fame, this view has never approved itself to the reflexion of philosophers, we may, while admitting that to some natures it deserves a high place in the hierarchy of goods, dismiss its claim to be considered the *summum bonum*.

Wisdom.—In knowledge we have the highest exercise of the highest faculty of man, and wisdom is the widest and fullest kind of knowledge. It is not surprising therefore to find philosophers regarding wisdom as the *summum bonum*, the most absolutely desirable end. But when we reflect, it seems that there is an end which makes wisdom thus desirable; we desire wisdom because it is, *ex hypothesi*, the highest excellence of our nature. And then the question arises, whether the intellectual faculty is really the highest, whether right acting will not claim the precedence over right thinking. There is on the whole a marked agreement to the effect that practice is the more important, though not perhaps the more characteristically human, and that wisdom is chiefly valuable as a means to practice. Occasionally, indeed, one hears from men of science unguarded expressions which would make the possession, or even the pursuit, of knowledge superior to all other goods; but these are, perhaps, not to be taken too seriously.

§ 3. Happiness.

The average plain man regards happiness as a good of the highest kind. He is prepared to admit, with Butler, that " our ideas of happiness are of all ideas the nearest and most important to us," and that " when we sit down in a cool hour we can neither justify to ourselves this or any other pursuit, till we are convinced that it will be for our happiness, or at least not contrary to it" (Sermon XI.).

The difficulty lies in the attempt to define happiness. It is commonly identified with pleasure and the absence of pain. This is the meaning attached to it by Locke ("Essay," bk. ii., ch. xxi., § 42) and Paley ("Moral Philos.," bk. i., chap. vi.), and it of course causes happiness to disappear from the list of competitors for the position of *summum bonum* in favour of pleasure.

There is however another view, specially associated

with the name of Aristotle, which defines happiness as an activity of the soul, such that its own special excellence is realized or fulfilled. It is at once well-being and well-doing. The greatest happiness lies in the best possible exercise of the highest faculties of our nature. Since the highest activity of the highest function is assumed to be accompanied by the highest pleasure,[1] if we lay stress on the pleasurableness, the feeling itself as opposed to its objective conditions, Aristotle's view tends to become purely hedonistic. But the assumption is certainly open to question. The pleasures of eating and drinking, to speak of no other animal satisfactions, appear to be judged by the majority of even highly intellectual and cultivated men as more intense, more capable of repetition and prolongation and more easily accessible than those of intellectual or moral exertion. They are perhaps even no more "impure" (that is, free from unpleasant accompaniments or consequences); since few men find study and philanthropic work free from constant weariness and disappointment. That Aristotle's theory does not become merely hedonistic, is partly due to almost inevitable confusion between pleasurable feeling and its intellectually perceived conditions, and partly due to the philosopher's unwillingness to purchase consistency at the expense of half the truth. As a matter of fact happiness does seem to involve an element which, while of the nature of feeling, is yet some-

---

[1] It is questionable whether Aristotle distinguishes between greatest and best pleasure.

thing more than mere pleasurableness. To distinguish this element is a task of considerable difficulty.

It seems to be best expressed by the word satisfaction or contentment; while ordinarily, pleasure means enjoyment without the necessary presupposition of a want, which is now fulfilled. This satisfaction or contentment is of a very general kind. It involves the previous occurrence of wants and their present fulfilment, and so, like many other ideas, contains an element of self-contradiction, viz., the pre-existence of a condition which is now removed. At the same time it is not the mere pleasure due to the fulfilment of wants; the amount of happiness does not depend on the number and intensity of our previous wants. Happiness consists largely in the satisfaction of needs for activity which, even when gratified, leave no strong sense of definite pleasure or enjoyment. This side of the conception is emphasized by John Grote in his "Moral Ideals" (pp. 291 *seq.*): "It is not 'the abundance of the things which he possesseth' which makes a man's life, but it is his *living*, his exercising his faculties; his happiness is his εὐπραξία, that word which the Greek moral instinct may almost be said to have made for the Aristotelic philosophy, in which feeling and action are joined in a single motive as they are joined in consciousness . . . . and this is the important or fundamental happiness."

Another distinction between happiness and pleasure is sometimes made. "Pleasure is the feeling which accompanies the satisfaction of particular desires; happiness is the feeling which accompanies the sense that, apart from the satisfaction of momentary desires, and even in spite of the pain of refusal and failure to satisfy them, the self as a whole is being realized."[1]

This view is unsatisfactory because it assumes the existence of a shadowy metaphysical self which is something distinct from the pure self and the empirical self; something which is neither the transcendental subject of thought pre-supposed in every intellectual activity, nor the phenomenal object of thought built up in antithesis to the external world. And unsatisfactory because it further involves the vague notion of the "realization" of this non-existent product of metaphysical subtlety.

§ 4. Pleasure.

Although the ordinary man accepts happiness as one of the highest goods, and even as the supreme good, he often shrinks from the plain statement that good is pleasure and evil is pain, which most philosophers regard as the logical outcome of the doctrine.

The charm of this identification lies in its extreme clearness and simplicity. It must seem to many students difficult to explain how Plato, after laying down with great precision in the "Protagoras" the doctrine that pleasure is the ultimate meaning of good,

---

[1] See Muirhead, "Elements of Ethics," p. 97.

should have abandoned it for the vague idealistic speculations of the later dialogues; and since his time nearly all ethical writers who have been remarkable for clearness and consistency of speculation rather than for breadth and subtlety, have been attracted by it. "Things are good or evil only in reference to pleasure or pain. That we call 'good' which is apt to cause or increase pleasure or diminish pain in us," directly or indirectly. ("Essay," bk. ii. ch. xx.) So certain has the identification of the one ultimate good with pleasure seemed to most of those who accept it, that they have quite commonly thought that it needed no proof at all.[1] They have regarded it as axiomatic. But when stated, their reasons appear somewhat less overwhelming than might have been expected.

Mill's proof of hedonism is thus expressed. "The only proof capable of being given that an object is visible is that people actually see it. The only proof that a sound is audible, is that people hear it: and so of the other sources of our experience. In like manner, I apprehend, the sole evidence it is possible to produce that anything is desirable, is that people do actually desire it" ("Utilitarianism," pp. 52-53). Thus having proved that pleasure is desirable, he goes on to demonstrate that nothing else is desired except in so far as it is pleasant. This he bases on the psychological doctrine that pleasure is the only object of desire, which he proves in turn by an appeal

[1] "So obvious does this appear to me that I expect it will hardly be disputed" (Mill, "Utilitarianism," p. 59).

to introspection and observation. "I believe that these sources of evidence impartially consulted will declare that desiring a thing and finding it pleasant, aversion to it and thinking of it as painful, are phenomena entirely inseparable .... in strictness of language two different modes of naming the same psychological fact" ("Utilitarianism," p. 58). Mill lays down three propositions (1), that what is desired is necessarily desirable; (2), that only pleasure is desired; (3), that desire and experience of pleasure are absolutely the same thing looked at in two different ways. The last is an extraordinary overstatement, but as an examination of it would need an unnecessary incursion into Psychology we may dismiss it without further ado. As to the first, Mill has obviously been misled by a paltry verbal jingle. While visible means capable of being seen, and audible, capable of being heard, desirable does not mean capable of being desired, but intrinsically worthy of desire; what *ought* to be desired. It is not a mere analytic proposition like the others, but a synthetic proposition, and one which cannot be proved by any appeal to experience. The mere fact that all men do desire pleasure is no proof that the ideally wise and good man would desire it. So far, however, is it from being a fact that all men always do desire pleasure that it has been questioned whether any men ever do. What men primarily and normally desire is not pleasure, but objects.[1] We

---

[1] See Höffding, "Outlines of Psychology," trans., pp. 323, 324, and chap. vi. § 7 below.

may, it is true, learn to desire things on account of the feelings they produce in us, and not as at first without conscious reference to our feelings; but even then what we desire is not pleasure. Pleasure is a mere abstraction, a quality of feeling mentally isolated from the feeling itself; and what we desire even in this further stage is the feeling and not the pleasantness of the feeling.

Dr. Sidgwick has given another proof of the hedonistic position.[1] His argument consists of three steps. First, he identifies good with excellence of human existence; secondly, he identifies excellence of human existence with excellence of conscious life; and thirdly, he identifies excellence of conscious life with pleasure. The first step may pass without challenge, since we have accepted this limitation above (§ 1). And we may allow that excellence of human existence does necessarily imply a reference to conscious life. The third proposition is at once the most important and most difficult to prove. Conscious life involves much more besides feeling, which alone possesses the quality of pleasurableness. Even if pleasure be the only desirable feature in feeling it is not thereby the only really desirable feature in conscious life. There remain those large departments of consciousness called intellect and will. But Dr. Sidgwick appeals to reflection, to the intuitive judgment of his readers, to decide whether "the objective relations of the conscious subject" which we call "cognition of Truth, contemplation

---

[1] "Methods of Ethics," book i. chap. ix.; book iii. chap. xiv.

of Beauty, Freedom of action," are in themselves desirable apart from the pleasure accompanying them. He adds that it still seems to him that "we can only justify to ourselves the importance that we attach to any of these objects by considering its conduciveness, in one way or another, to the happiness of sentient beings." My own reflection does not seem sufficiently consistent to rely much on its deliverances, but on the whole it seems to be adverse to Dr. Sidgwick. Many plain men as well as philosophers would hold with Kant that the good will is a good apart from the pleasure it brings to us or to others.

But the plausibility of Mill's and of Dr. Sidgwick's view really comes from their definition of pleasure as preferable feeling. It is clear that the one really desirable consciousness is pleasure, if we have defined pleasure as that consciousness which is desirable. Pleasure, according to Dr. Sidgwick, means desirable consciousness, that is, the consciousness which it is reasonable to desire and seek. To say, then, that it is reasonable to seek pleasure, is to say that it is reasonable to desire the consciousness which it is reasonable to desire (Green, "Prolegomena to Ethics," p. 410). To sum up, Professor Sidgwick reduces good to goodness of consciousness; he gets rid of the element of objective relation in consciousness (cognition and will), and identifies goodness of consciousness with goodness of feeling; he interprets good feeling as preferable feeling, and says that by pleasure he means preferable feeling.

And remember that "pleasure" is ambiguous. When we call any of our sensations pleasurable, we imply a certain definite quality of feeling, which is something more than mere preferableness. But in speaking of the higher feelings, pleasurable means merely preferable, that is, what will be preferred by all really good and wise men.

§ 5. Excellence or Perfection.

If excellence is desirable then perfection, as the highest conceivable excellence, must be still more desirable. At least this is true when we look at the sum of faculties; though in the case of any one faculty, or group of faculties, it may be often the case that we should regard excellence beyond a certain point as undesirable, simply because a higher degree of excellence would involve the neglect or stunting of other faculties of equal or greater importance. This exception being noted, we shall assume that excellence as an aim practically involves perfection.

Physical, intellectual, and moral excellence are all, *primâ facie*, desirable. Is desirability the only common link, or can we resolve one into the other? It has often been assumed that the *corpus sanum* is only good in so far as it is a necessary condition of the *mens sana*, and this latter again only in so far as it is a condition of the completest moral goodness. But modern writers do not always admit this, and there is perhaps a tendency to regard all three as absolutely choiceworthy. The evolutionists, for instance, do not seem to have seriously considered the possibility of their being permanently and ultimately in rivalry. But most philosophers assume that "Virtues are the chief of human perfections," and other perfections are strictly subordinate to these.

Dr. Sidgwick argues from this that perfection cannot be the *summum bonum*. For it will imply the determination of what *is* virtuous by some standard outside perfection itself. Perfection means moral perfection, and moral perfection means action in accordance with a standard of good conduct, which must be something else than perfection itself, or we shall have a *circulus in definiendo*. To this some moralists, *e.g.*, Green, would reply that such a circulus is inevitable, whatever standard we adopt.[1] Others would say that moral perfection consists, not in doing good acts, but in the will to do them. It is the good-will itself which constitutes the moral excellence, and therefore there is no real need to assume an extrinsic standard of goodness at all. As long as we want to do what we believe to be right, it does not matter what we *do* believe to be right. But this is too much at variance with common sense, which refuses to recognize moral perfection in Torquemadas and Robespierres, however single in aim and consistent in life.

Others, again, would say that as good is the objective fact answering to want, so the *summum bonum*

---

[1] "Prolegomena," pp. 204 *seq.*

will be what satisfies the highest want. But this answer leaves us with the difficulty of determining what is our highest want. We may say that those wants are the highest which belong to us *quâ* man, those which belong to our intellectual, artistic, and moral nature. But we do not seem to have any clear criterion to settle the relative claims between these three classes of wants. It does not appear that a moral need, *e.g.*, desire for peace and for reconciliation with others, is always and necessarily higher than an intellectual or æsthetic one. Again, the evolutionary theory does not supply us with a means of defining "highest want" without in any way implying the idea of good which we are seeking to define by means of "highest want."

Another and more successful attempt to define perfection without assuming the idea of moral excellence is found in the theory which substitutes social welfare for excellence or happiness.

This, like Aristotle's εὐδαιμονία, really embraces both ideas. The substitution of it for the somewhat more definite terms is due chiefly to biological analogies. With Mr. Leslie Stephen social welfare practically means social health. "The existence of the social tissue at any stage of development, and its power of maintaining itself, either as a part of the special order or as against other societies, depends essentially upon the fulfilment of certain conditions. Since the qualities by which societies differ do not depend upon the innate qualities of its constituent members, which remain constant (or approximately constant) through long periods of social development, but upon these qualities as modified and developed by means of the social factors, it follows again that the society grows on condition of impressing a certain character upon its members. This takes place in the earlier stages by the development of a social sentiment unfavourable to certain specific modes of conduct. As the society becomes more reasonable, more capable of understanding and applying general principles, the sentiment develops into an approval of a certain type of character, the existence of which fits the individual for membership of a thoroughly efficient and healthy social tissue. . . . Briefly, then, we may say that morality is a statement of the conditions of social welfare; and morality, as distinguished from prudence, refers to those conditions which imply a direct action upon the social union. In other words, morality is the sum of the preservative instincts of a society, and presumably of those which imply a desire for the good of the society itself."[1]

This really leaves the denotation of welfare unsettled. "Efficient tissue" is tissue efficient for some end. The instincts which make for the preservation of a society must make for the existence in the society of some special conditions or qualities, unless the mere existence of the society is conceived as sufficient. Otherwise the εὖ ζῆν is resolved into the ζῆν;

---

[1] Leslie Stephen, "Science of Ethics," pp. 215 *seq.*

and so Mr. Spencer speaks of "that increased duration of life which constitutes the supreme end."[1]

Mr. Alexander substitutes for welfare the still less determinate notion of Equilibrium of the Social Order. He calls conduct good or bad as it leads to social equilibrium. "Good and bad acts and conduct are distinguished by their adjustment, or failure of adjustment, to the social order."[2]

§ 6. The Summum Bonum.

But even if moral goodness can be determined apart from one of the other methods, and we can thus regard moral excellence as a *summum bonum*, is it the only *summum bonum*? Shall we, instead of a single system, have several systems of goods, each leading to the excellence of some department of human life, but none capable of subordinate relation to any of the others?

We recognize the need to weigh good things against each other. Not only do we weigh obviously relative goods, *e.g.*, two residences against each other, but even such quasi-absolute goods as life, health, and spiritual well-being are constantly compared. Even the good man may measure against each other without any strong feeling of absurdity or degradation the relative advan-

---

[1] Spencer, "Principles of Ethics," vol. i., p. 14. This expression is, however, not easily reconcilable with other passages of a more hedonistic character.

[2] Alexander, "Moral Order and Progress," p. 127.

tages of a larger income on the one hand and increased educational and religious opportunities for himself and his family on the other; and while he might decide in favour of the latter if the increase of income was a matter of £50 a year, might hesitate if it was a matter of £500. Much more difficult is the position when we have to weigh physical health of oneself or others against our own, or their, moral improvement. And more difficult still when the rival goods are knowledge, or artistic creation, and moral activity. At first sight, no doubt, we admire the man who seeks at any cost the "one thing needful." But on reflection it does not seem that we should be able to say decisively that intellectual and æsthetic progress must always give way to moral. We should not be willing to purchase a small increase of virtue at the expense of a great increase of Puritan asceticism; to destroy our picture-galleries and theatres, our novels and poems, in one great bonfire of vanities. Could Romola really wish any more than Monna Brigida that all the world should turn *piagnoni?* Should we be willing to substitute for Shakespeare another St. Francis?

The natural instinct of good men seems to assume that the various kinds of human perfection, although rivals, are yet not absolutely exclusive of each other.

"That Beauty, Good, and Knowledge are three sisters
That doat upon each other."

If this be so we may have to do away with the idea of a single *summum bonum* altogether (unless we can find one which shall embrace all three), and substitute for it the conception of a cycle of ends, a self-supporting system of goods.

Early speculation always tends to arrange its notions in the form of a single series. The earth rests on an elephant, the elephant on a tortoise. It then seeks to complete the series by placing an absolute term, a staple in the wall from which the chain of causation, or the chain of goods, may depend. The material universe is rounded off by the *primum mobile;* the ethical cosmos is completed by the *summum bonum.* Modern thought tends to replace this hierarchical organisation by a more democratic one. The solar system is to us self-supporting; each part of it is concerned in the perpetuation of the whole. The organs and functions of the animal body are not arrayed serially and hierarchically, but form a circle of mutually interacting organs, each of which is in turn supreme and subaltern. We no longer dispute as to which is logically prior, the egg or the hen; but we regard each as necessarily involving the other. In the cycle of seed, plant, flower, fruit, seed, we may begin anywhere, and regard that term (for our special purpose) as ultimate; but we know that this is due only to a practical necessity, or a logical artifice, and that no one term is really absolute while the rest are only relative to it. In metaphysics, again, the tendency is no longer to search for an absolute criterion and basis in some one principle, as Descartes did, but to regard the whole of knowledge as a system of mutually supporting truths, each of which derives its validity from its compatibility with all the rest.

May we not expect to find that in the same way the whole of human life is the end of the whole; that there is no interest absolutely final and independent of the others; that goodness is to be found in whatever furthers the whole or any part of the whole, so long as it does not interfere with the existence of the rest? Some interests are clearly subordinate, in the sense that their main importance is derived from their contributory relation to some other interest. Health is thus in the main subordinate to happiness and bodily perfection; but can we rightfully say that Truth, or Beauty, or Virtue, should ever be eliminated from human existence, in order to further one of the competing goods? The truly wise man will not seek to attain a facile unity of purpose by the denial and suppression of the rival ideals; he will seek, though often unsuccessfully, to reconcile them, trusting that as the world progresses a higher and completer conciliation will be possible than his rough and empirical one; but knowing, too, that the crudest effort at synthesis is more likely to be right than an attempt to simplify the problem by omitting half of the terms.

On this view the whole of human life is good, the parts only good by reference to the whole; yet the goodness of the whole can perhaps only be expressed as the sum of the goodness of the parts.

§ 7. Humanity.

The Comtists have put forward humanity as the end of rational action. But this theory comes practically to altruistic hedonism.

"Rational nature exists as an end in itself," says Kant, and he identifies rational nature with humanity. This identification is open to question, unless we are willing to take up a definitely atheistic or agnostic position, since rational nature must include God and possible other supra-human beings. Putting aside this objection, there is the farther difficulty that Kant identifies humanity with the practical reason, mere formal will without content.

But if we interpret "humanity" in a concrete sense, as the whole sum of human existence, we are perhaps led back to the end already discussed, viz., excellence, which again we saw naturally resolved itself into perfection of human existence. It is not, however, quite clear that we are bound to interpret excellence always as perfection (see § 5, above). It may be urged that we have no right to try to eliminate any fact in human nature merely because it interferes with the greatest possible sum total of perfection. It may be said that Kant's rule, "So act as to treat humanity, whether in thine own person or in that of any other, in every case as an end, never as simply a means," is a warning to the idealist as well as the hedonist. We have no right to treat humanity simply as material on which to impress our own high purposes. No ideal is absolute.

Above all ideals stands humanity. If our efforts on behalf of any ideal conflict irreconcilably with any part of the aggregate of interests and energies which constitute human consciousness, we have no right to sacrifice the latter to the former. We must not destroy art, culture, and enjoyment for the sake of religion or of freedom; nor freedom or religion for the sake of art and culture.

This view brings us again to the notion of the *summum bonum*, not as a *summum genus* under which all other *bona* stand; but as a cycle of *bona*, which are partly independent, in so far as they cannot be adequately expressed in terms of each other.

§ 8. God.

Some Christian writers advance the theory that God is the ultimate end of all rational conduct. But life for God and desire of Him seem to be metaphorical expressions. We can live in obedience to the divine commands with desire to please Him, and earnestly hoping to participate in the life of higher blessedness which He has promised. We cannot possibly make Him an end in the same way as we can Fame, Pleasure, or Perfection.

Modern theologians would probably attach only a metaphorical meaning to such expressions as the "non aliam [mercedem] nisi te, Domine," of St. Thomas Aquinas.

With the majority of Christians and even of theologians, the one supreme good is described, not as the possession of God, but as the enjoyment of the "exceeding great rewards He has prepared for them that love Him." This view is of course really hedonistic.

There is need to determine the fundamental notions of ethics without having recourse to theological ideas. If duty and ethics are to exist for those who do not accept monotheism, we must not base our morality on a system which they have never heard of, or do not believe. The very assertion that it is our duty to seek for God implies the antecedent determination of the idea of duty. And the ascription to Him of ethical attributes implies that a meaning attaches to these independently of theological beliefs.

§ 9. Good as essentially relative.

It is perhaps best to allow that good is an essentially relative term. This is obviously so, if, as Socrates held,[1] good denotes always what is useful as a means. Even if we accept the view put forward in § 1 of this chapter, we must regard Good as relative. The judgment that "this is good," is the intellectual expression of a desire. Now such a desire always starts from a definite set of circumstances; what is

[1] See Xenophon, "Memorabilia," II. viii.; cf. Gizycki and Coit, p. 6.

desirable is desirable only under conditions. There is no absolutely desirable thing.

"Nothing is good I see without respect," says Portia ("Merchant of Venice," v. 1), meaning without relation.[1]

Again, we can never come to the end of desire, as long as consciousness exists. No matter what is attained desire still remains, and with it the judgment that something (else) is good. We can never say, "This is the final good on which all the rest depend; if we have this we have all." Such an assertion is as unmeaning as the statement that here, or here, is the boundary of space. Space has only meaning for us as far as it is limited, but every bound implies a further space beyond it. So too with cause. An absolute first cause, and an absolute final cause are both unmeaning to us as philosophers. It is only from the point of view of theology that absolute meaning can be attached to any category of thought.

We may, perhaps, seem to come near finding an absolute good in the cycle of ends of highest rank (§ 6), the system of supreme human interests. But we cannot say that the particular goods in this cycle gain their desirability from each other, or from the cycle as a whole. We can only say that a man's good lies in the attainment of a number of different ends, some of which are in partial antagonism, but none of which can be reasonably omitted by the normally constituted

[1] Compare Hamlet's, "There is nothing good or bad but thinking makes it so" (ii. 2).

man as an an object of interest and effort. This complete attainment is *ex hypothesi* impossible, since they are not entirely consistent. And thus good still remains, though in a different sense, a relative term.

CHAPTER III.

RIGHT, OBLIGATION, DUTY.

§ 1. Right.

THE term Right, which has played in the history of English ethics a still more important part than the term Good, although not borrowed from Law, at any rate when used as an adjective, yet implies what may be called a jural view of morality. It suggests that the propositions of ethics are not so much judgments as rules with which we must comply. It implies a definite standard, which can be approximated to but not transcended. In the recognition of conduct as right we have a positive notion which, in the strict sense of the term, is incapable of degrees, while we can call it good in various degrees. Right does not admit of comparison in the same way as good. It is, however, worth while to notice, that conduct which is not right is not necessarily *wrong*, any more than conduct which is not good is bad. It is simply not right. But when we deal with the other end of the scale the difference comes in; your conduct cannot be more than right, it may be more than good, viz., the best.

This difference implies that the standard of right is

more definite than that of good. Indeed, when we speak of conduct as right we imply a more intellectual attitude towards moral problems; the conduct is or is not in accordance with a principle rationally apprehended. When we speak of conduct as good we imply a more emotional attitude, the feeling of approval is more prominent, the rigid alternative of inclusion within or exclusion from a particular category is no longer before us.

But this very precise usage of right is constantly laid aside. In practice we often assume degrees of right. From the grudging admission that "it is right enough," which indicates that a given act is just in accordance with what society demands, to the assertion that it is perfectly right, there is a long step. The word right implies a standard, but not always the same standard.

Another distinction may be drawn between right and good conduct. The former is always within our power, the latter is not. This distinction, however, depends on confusion between the formal and material aspects of rightness. Materially right conduct, conduct which is right without reference to us, is often no more in our power than good conduct. We may have to choose between two evils, for instance, between doing something unkind or unworthy on the one hand, and breaking a promise on the other hand. One of the two may be right for us, but neither course is right in the widest sense.

§ 2. The Standard of Right.

By right, as an adjective, we mean what is in accordance with the standard of conduct which for the time we accept. This may be *legal*, or *social*, or that which we regard as the *ideal moral* standard. Conduct may comply with the demands of law, or of social custom, without being, as we say, morally right.

The ideally correct conduct is assumed to have some sort of objective reality. It is independent of the wishes of the individual. It is valid for anyone else in exactly the same circumstances as myself. It is in accordance with the standard of excellence recognized by the ideally just and wise man, *i.e.*, by a judgment determined in its conclusion by no merely egoistic or other partial considerations, but by full and complete knowledge of and complete regard for all interests involved.

Right conduct, then, is in the highest sense of the term reasonable conduct. But it is difficult to define reasonable satisfactorily without reference to some objective standard. Reasonable conduct is conduct which is not only dictated by reason, but by reason acting validly, *i.e.* rightly. The only way of escape from this circle seems to be in the reference to the φρόνιμος of Aristotle, which, however, moves the difficulty only a little further back.

Some moralists, for instance Kant, have asserted that there is no criterion of material rightness—that no act is morally right except such as is done for the formal principle of rightness, viz., a desire to do right because it is right. This view pushed to its logical conclusion makes the positive content of morality unimportant. I may commit murder or suicide from a desire to do right as such; and my act will be not only praiseworthy but right. On the other hand I may relieve the miserable and comfort the afflicted, and my act be of no higher moral worth than the act of the burglar and the hired assassin. But these conclusions are revolting to common sense as well as moral feeling. We cannot help assuming a certain objectivity in our moral ideas, as well as in our æsthetic ideas. The music of the savages who beat tom-toms gives them as much pleasure as a symphony of Beethoven gives us, and much more than such a symphony would give them; but we do not allow that the two performances are equally beautiful, or even equally pleasurable. We are obliged to allow that pleasure is the main determining factor in our judgment of æsthetic effects. But we refuse to allow that the pleasure of the savage is of equal æsthetic validity with our own. In the same way, we allow that moral effort is of primary importance in the production of a *really* moral act; but we do not allow that every act which is done from a pure sense of duty is equally good and right. We cannot help assuming that there is some objective standard. A king of Dahomey, who, actuated by a conscious desire to act justly and properly, tortures to death the requisite number of victims on the grave of his predecessor, is no doubt, from the subjective and formal point of view, superior to a king who from mere laziness fails to do so. But we cannot bring ourselves to leave out of account the "content" of the act; and to put this case on the same level as if the matter in which he excelled had been the erection of a hospital to assist the injured and suffering.

§ 3. Rights.

The word right is used substantively as well as adjectivally. A right is a legal, or quasi-legal, term, correlative to an obligation. A right to do this vested in me, is simply an obligation on the part of others not to interfere with me while I do it. This right, and the correlative obligation, are the creation of law, and imply the existence of law. If we extend the idea of law into the realm of ethics, and look at moral truths under the aspect of laws, we may metaphorically speak of a moral right and a moral obligation.[1]

The legal and the ethical sense have not been kept apart, and have reacted on each other. Writers have not sufficiently realized that such terms as "natural rights" have a purely metaphorical meaning. A right is a creation of law, and has no meaning apart from law. But by a natural extension of meaning it connotes a liberty which is the correlative of some obligation not actually imposed by law, but supposed to be imposed by God's law, *i.e.*, the metaphysical God of ideal morality.

[1] See Austin, "Lect. on Jurisprudence," vol. i., p. 354; also p. 293, note. See Raleigh's "Elementary Politics," pp. 68, *seq.*

The natural rights are those supposed to be conferred apart from and prior to any actual human law, *i.e.*, those belonging to man as man. This of course carries us back to the theories of the Greek philosophers and Roman lawyers which still maintain a half-vitalized sort of existence in the minds of plain men.[1]

Such rights and obligations are said to be *imperfect*, because they cannot be enforced judicially. Strictly speaking they are not rights at all, in the sense in which legal rights are such. They are not "conferred by commands issuing from the sovereign." But the metaphorical use, understood as such, is a very convenient one, and may very properly be retained.

Yet we must be careful to remember that a natural right is something very different from a legal right. What the ideal law of nature orders cannot be determined precisely, because there is no such thing as a law of nature in this sense of the term. It means such a law as would exist in an ideal society, where everybody did his duty, and where actual law was not obliged to limp a long way after morality. A natural right to property or to freedom is an ethical or political fiction.

§ 4. Jus Naturale.

By Natural Law or Law of Nature in the ethical or quasi-legal sense we mean something quite different from a scientific law. A law of nature in the scientific

[1] See end of § 6 below.

sense is a highly general uniformity which has been observed to occur among phenomena; *e.g.*, the law of gravitation. The only link of meaning between such laws and political laws lies (1) in their generality—they apply to everything of the same kind—and (2) in the implicit assumption that they are given as commands by the Creator. This latter suggestion is obviously extremely inaccurate; since matter is not intelligent and self-directive and cannot in any exact sense be said to obey, or even to receive commands. The relation between God and the created universe can only by the roughest figurative language be likened to the relation between a sovereign law-giver and his subjects.

The Stoics, whose teaching approached more nearly that of the early church than did the teaching of any other philosophical sect then existing, taught a sort of pantheism. The energy which lies behind phenomena is God; in a very real sense the world is a manifestation of God. Each of us is a part of this ordered universe, and to live according to nature meant to live in agreement with the nature of God as exhibited in the external universe and in the mind of man. The Roman moralists were nearly all Stoics, and Stoical elements were worked into the tissue of the new Roman law.[1] The magistrates who had been forming a working code for intercourse between Roman citizens and foreigners by selecting the rules of law common to Rome and to

[1] Maine, "Ancient Law," chap. iii. See below, chap. v., § 8.

the different Italian communities, called it the *jus gentium*. "The *jus naturale* is simply the *jus gentium* seen in the light of a particular theory," viz., the Stoic theory of the divine origin of nature and of law. "After Nature had become a household word in the mouths of the Romans, the belief gradually prevailed among the Roman lawyers that the old *Jus Gentium* was in fact the lost code of Nature, and that the Prætor in framing an edictal jurisprudence on the principles of the *Jus Gentium* was gradually restoring a type from which law had only departed to deteriorate." This conception of an ideal law, antecedent and superior to the positive law, universally valid and binding on everybody even when free from the restrictions of positive law, has given us the great system of Roman Law, the modern codes built on it, and the system of International Law; and it is the basis of the ethical intuitionism of Butler and Kant, and of the revolutionary morality of Rousseau. To Rousseau, again, may be traced the crude political theories of modern democracy. The doctrine of the "rights of man" given and guaranteed by Nature is the central dogma of Liberalism.

§ 5. Obligation.

The idea of obligation involves the subjection of our wills to a law. It further suggests that there is some possible conflict between our motives, though this is no necessary part of the meaning.

The jurisprudential school of utilitarians, such as

Bentham and Austin, have resolved obligation into a purely positive idea; according to them it expresses the fact that we are liable to some penalty if we disobey the command of another. This penalty they call the " sanction."[1]

The word obligation thus primarily expresses the positive relation of the subject to the law of his sovereign : it is a strictly legal term. But by extension of meaning it may be applied to the analogous relation of the individual to the code of rules which society enforces, positive morality. The sanction here is no longer a penalty formally inflicted by a special officer; but the more indefinite punishment due to the bad opinion of others, together with the reproaches of those who have any recognized right to interfere with us (*e.g.*, relatives, spiritual superiors, schoolmasters). This is the " social sanction," or, as Bentham calls it, " moral sanction."

By a further extension of the meaning of the word obligation, it is made to cover the relation of the indi-

---

[1] " The pain or pleasure which is attached to a law, forms what is called its sanction" (Bentham). On the other hand, Austin restricts the term to mean the " evil (*i.e.* pain) which will probably be incurred in case a command be disobeyed."

Bentham distinguishes four kinds of Sanctions :—
  (1) *Physical*—due to nature, acting without human intervention.
  (2) *Moral*—or social—due to the spontaneous disposition of our fellow-men, their friendship, hatred, esteem, etc.
  (3) *Political*—or legal—due to the action of the magistrate in virtue of the laws.
  (4) *Religious*.

vidual to the ideal moral code conceived as God's law, whether enforced by society or not. The sanction in this case will be God's rewards and punishments in this life and the next. Thus even if society will not frown on some secret sin, the obligation to abstain from it exists. Besides the *ab extra* rewards and punishments which God is supposed to affix to the commission of offences against the ideal moral law, there are the pleasures and pains of conscience; the inner moral sanction (which Bentham characteristically overlooks). My reason recognizes the law and recognizes that it applies to me; my moral feelings thereupon urge me to act in accordance with it. The pain which will arise if these feelings are injured, the pleasure which will arise if they are gratified, are a powerful sanction.

But it would seem that the moral obligation itself does not arise from the pain or pleasure. I recognize that I am bound, and the feeling follows. The analysis of Bentham and Austin which makes the notion of obligation involve that of sanction, is untenable. The obligation expresses the relation of my will to the law; when I know that my particular case is included under the law, that the law applies to me, I know that I am bound, and all that the notion of obligation involves is present. Alongside of this judgment spring up the moral feelings, the desire to do right as such, and other emotions; but the existence of these feelings does not constitute the fact of obligation.

What reason recognizes as moral truth is also moral law. The ideal reason recognizes this course as the proper course for me. This course, then, is incumbent on me. Moral obligation is constituted not by the fact of pains and pleasures naturally or artificially attached to my conduct; but by the fact that I am a rational being and capable of directing my acts in accordance with reason. I may not yet recognize the law, but ὁ φρόνιμος will recognize it; and I may by education at any time be brought to recognize it.

This is what Kant calls the *Categorical imperative.* Other imperatives are more or less conditional. If in any art we wish to produce a certain effect, say a good picture or a savoury dish, we are obliged to adopt certain necessary means; our obligation is strictly relative, since the end itself is not necessarily desired. This is called a technical imperative, for such are the rules of the various arts. Another kind of hypothetical imperative is (perhaps unnecessarily) distinguished by Kant. If we recognize that a certain action is necessary to secure something on which our happiness depends, our obligation to perform it is still a conditional one, since we perform the action only as a means to the end of happiness; but as, according to Kant, we necessarily and inevitably desire our own happiness, this imperative is no longer merely problematic but assertorial. The end (unlike the production of the picture or the dish) is not one which we may wish to realize, but one which we always do and indeed must wish to realize. The counsels of prudence, or rules for prudent conduct, belong to this type of imperative. In antithesis to these two kinds of hypothetical commands Kant places the categorical imperative of morality, which is unconditional. It is binding on us without reference to any consequences. It is an absolute imperative.[1]

§ 6. Duty.

Duty denotes the aggregate of acts prescribed by moral law, everything that I ought to do. Any part of this aggregate may be described as a duty. That part which lies nearest to hand is emphatically " our duty." In a certain sense all moral acts which I can do are duties. But as a matter of fact we usually employ the word to denote those moral acts which we are liable to leave undone. " What duty is cannot be understood without a law," says Locke. It implies conscious reference to an accepted standard of conduct. Obligation is the attitude we hold towards the law; duty indicates the substance of the law itself.

Duties are moral acts sanctioned by pleasures and pains of conscience. They are moral acts viewed as requiring the special stimulus of the moral sanction. This is due to the suggestion underlying the word

---

[1] Kant's categorical imperative runs in this form: "Act only on that maxim [or principle of action] which thou canst will should become a universal law." See his "Metaphysic of Morals," Sect. II. (translated by T. K. Abbott). Professor Sidgwick gives a sufficient account in his "History of Ethics."

"obligation," viz., that we shall not always find our impulses in accordance with reason.

If we look at some act of beneficence to our children as prescribed by reason, and as one which we are likely to be somewhat unwilling to fulfil, we call it a duty. If we look at it as natural and in accordance with our wishes, we do not call it a duty; we do not, in fact, consider it from point of view of morality at all. It is done so easily as not to challenge reflection. Ought never occurs to us in the matter. If we look at it as requiring more than average strength of character and goodness of disposition, we call it a virtuous act. It all depends, then, on the way we look at the act. Viewed *sub specie juris,* from the judicial or forensic point of view (as it will be if we are tempted to omit it), it is duty; viewed as natural and requiring no special effort, it is thought objectively of without reference to ourselves and is brought under no moral category; viewed *sub specie perfectionis,* as a difficult and exceptional act, it is virtuous.

Since duty and obligation express the relation of the objective law to our subjective and imperfect wills, they suggest, as has been said, the notion of conflict and effort. Duty is a standard to which we try to rise, but may fail to reach.

Since the content of any moral rule looked at as binding on us may be regarded as a duty, the possibility of a conflict of duties resolves itself into the possibility of a conflict of moral rules. If we pay no regard to the special circumstances of the individual, two or more courses of action may seem incumbent on him, which may yet be mutually conflicting, " incompossible " as Hamilton would have said. But we must believe that to the ideally wise man, ὁ φρόνιμος, this conflict will disappear. For me here and now only one course is the best, though it may be very little the best, and may involve the omission of some other good or the doing of some evil. Unfortunately in practice the ideal sage is usually absent, and we must content ourselves with only a rough decision, which leaves the conflict prominent. To aim at the highest benevolence within our reach often involves disregard of the highest justice or of truth. We are in the position of a judge forced to decide between apparently contradictory statutes or rules of procedure. We must either ignore one of them entirely, or make an attempt to conciliate the rival principles.

In such cases we cannot come to any satisfactory decision as long as we feel bound to consider the morality *sub specie juris.* Instead of rules we must have principles; we must have virtues instead of duties. The ideally perfect painter will see that to a given problem of art there is one solution which will give the complete answer. But to any short of the perfect artist, there may seem possible several solutions, none of them entirely satisfactory, because all of them will involve the disregarding of some one excellence in order to secure some other, or several others.

We are under no necessity to regard the moral precepts as rules, but nevertheless this category of duty is of supreme importance, especially to the young and impulsive. Few, indeed, are the

> " Glad hearts, without reproach or blot,
> Who do thy work and know it not!"

Most of us feel with the poet the need for the guidance and control which are to be found in rules. Looked at as a code, moral precepts are conceived as clear and explicit. We may break such rules, but we cannot do more than obey. "Thus while virtue is a scale rising indefinitely upwards, duty is the top of a scale descending downwards" (Grote, "Moral Ideals," ch. vii., p. 85). Again, while virtue is thought of merely as an attribute of the individual who exhibits it, duty is conceived as involving a law, which again seems to imply a law-giver whose command it is. This law-giver may be God, or society, or reason; but in any case the notion of duty is bilateral in a way that the notion of virtue is not. The man who does his duty is, even to Kant, obeying a command; he is as subject obeying himself, or rather impersonal reason, as legislator. The imperfect impulses of the empirical ego are conceived as obeying the law impersonal reason lays down. Indeed, the idea of duty often involves a third person, to whom the duty is owed. But John Grote is wrong in putting this too absolutely, for it only occurs when the conduct inspired by duty is itself essentially bilateral, *i.e.*, implies a patient as well as an agent. To abstain from intoxication may be regarded as a duty, but no third person seems here involved. To succour the afflicted may be regarded as a duty, but as it involves an afflicted person to be succoured, this conduct, viewed *sub specie juris*, takes the form of a *quasi*-debt, which I owe to the sufferer.

It is said that the notions of duty and obligation would not exist for a perfectly good will. "Evidently then with complete adaptation to the social state, that element of the moral consciousness which is expressed by the word 'obligation' will disappear" (Spencer). "A perfectly good will would therefore be equally subject to objective (moral) law, but could not be conceived as obliged thereby to act lawfully. . . . Ought is here out of place, because volition is already of itself necessarily in unison with the law" (Kant). But this suggests that the probability of conflict between our higher and lower nature is involved in the idea. No doubt the emotional concomitants of the idea are not entirely pleasant; a long experience has taught us how feeble is reason, and how strong are our other impulses. Still it does not seem necessary to assume that obligation is only possible when such conflict exists or may exist. For instance, *pace* Kant, it does not appear improper to say that God is obliged to act morally by His very nature. The distinction between the fact of obligation and the feeling which accompanies the recognition of obligation must be observed.

A distinction is sometimes made between duties of *perfect* and of *imperfect obligation*. But this is due to the unfortunate importation of a confusion from jurisprudence. In Roman law, laws of imperfect obligation are "laws which speak the desires of political superiors, but which their authors (by oversight or design) have not provided with sanction." Such imperfect laws are in reality not laws at all, but counsels or exhortations. They have, strictly speaking, *no* obligation. Some moralists have adopted the expression, and have given a new meaning to it. "Speaking of imperfect obligation, they commonly mean duties which are not legal, duties imposed by command of God, or duties imposed by positive morality, as contradistinguished to duties imposed by positive law." In this sense imperfect obligation means religious or moral obligation, as opposed to political (Austin, "Lect. on Jurisp.," vol. i., p. 102). Duties thus enforced by the machinery of government are sometimes called determinate, while the others are called indeterminate—*officia juris* and *officia virtutis*.

§ 7. Virtue.

We must distinguish between excellencies of conduct and excellencies of character which lead to the production of them. It is the latter which are properly called *virtues*. They are habits or tendencies of character which lead us to the performance of acts which are in accordance with the ideal of conduct formed by the best men of our time.[1] Such tenden-

---

[1] Cf. Aristotle, "Nic. Eth.," book ii., chap. vii.

cies are tendencies to act in a certain way and to feel in a certain way—the latter being a point somewhat overlooked by Aristotle—and they are acquired at any rate in part by practice of good acts, although they may be in some cases largely due to native endowment.

The term virtue is, however, sometimes applied to the *acts* themselves. It does not seem correct to say that this usage is metaphorical, and that " virtuous conduct means conduct which proves the virtue of the doer." A man is said to "make a virtue of necessity," and we call an act "virtuous," meaning that it is in accordance with the accepted ideals of conduct, or the demands of moral law. But in this use the word tends to be limited in its application to acts which are distinctly somewhat more excellent than those which are regarded as in the most stringent sense binding on all, to the class of acts which are called meritorious. We do not call paying our butcher's bill a virtuous act. In fact, in this usage of the term virtuous the idea of merit is involved, and when merit cannot be predicated, we do not speak of the act as virtuous. This, as we have seen, implies the jural view of ethics, but implies further that this view is transcended, that the prescriptions of moral law are not the ultimate possibilities of moral excellence.

Again, the terms virtuous and virtue, as applied to character, have each been restricted in popular usage to chastity, especially in regard to women, with regard to whom this particular excellence takes a very high, indeed the highest place. In the same way vice has been popularly used with special reference to bad sexual conduct. Moralists have hardly done their duty in so far as they have failed to point out the distorting effects on popular morality of this one-sided restriction.

§ 8. Merit.

An act which is of more than ordinary goodness is often called meritorious. The term implies either that the act is specially difficult to the ordinary man, or is specially difficult for the doer, and that therefore the moral law does not require the act, or, at any rate, not the degree of perfection in the act which is actually attained. This idea of merit obviously depends on the jural view of morality being taken, and stands in some opposition to duty. What duty requires strictly is not a source of merit; merit comes in where strict obligation no longer exists. If we comply with a higher law not rigidly binding on us we have merit or desert. This may be looked on as a sort of debt owed us by God, by the State, or by our fellow-men; who if they act justly will not only consider us free from desert of punishment, but as actually worthy of approval. But "in his own judgment a morally developed man does not inquire what will give him a claim to receive praise, but simply what is right; and he does not compare himself to others, but with his own moral ideal. Therefore, in reference to himself, he knows only duty, not desert" (Gizycki and Coit, p. 103).

§ 9. Responsibility.

Responsibility means answerableness. A man is responsible to his employers for his use of their money or goods; he can be called upon to give an account of that which has been entrusted to his care. By an extension of the idea we speak of a man's responsibility to a political superior for the employment of his time or activity. In this wide sense of the word, to say that a person is responsible is to say that he can be punished.

The conditions under which it is possible for a man to be legally responsible, *i.e.*, to be under legal obligation with regard to an act, are fixed somewhat arbitrarily by law. For instance, a man is sometimes held responsible for injury done to others by his servants, even if they are not acting on an implied command from him, thus in most countries an innkeeper is bound to make restitution for robberies committed by his servants, while this is not the case with other masters.[1] The conditions of *moral* responsibility, on the other hand, are determined by the psychological condition of the individual, without regard to consequences; hence moral and legal responsibility often rest on quite different persons.

[1] The object of the law is to bring pressure to bear on innkeepers to take the greatest care to ensure the honesty of their servants.

The conditions of moral responsibility seem to be:

(1) Knowledge of the nature and conditions of the act. This must be an actual present knowledge, and not a merely constructive knowledge. There must be full consciousness for responsibility to be complete. But yet we are obliged to assume that the temporary forgetfulness due to passion does not absolve. Strictly speaking we ought to say that a person who does wrong in a passion is not responsible for the act then committed, but for the original evil of getting into the passion. And so with regard to drunkenness; although "per vinum delapsis capitalis pœna remittitur," yet the original fault of taking too much wine is punishable. If a man produces mental disease by taking nervous stimulants, we do not hold him responsible for any further immoral act he may commit, but only for the course of conduct which made it possible or even probable.

(2) Knowledge of the rule which the act contravenes. Here there is divergence between legal and moral responsibility. Ignorance of the law does not excuse in law. But it certainly does in morality, subject to the same exceptions mentioned above, viz., that the ignorance be not itself due to our own fault.

(3) Power of choice. There must be no external compulsion, physical or mental. Compulsion may (it is usually said) take the form of (*a*) actual force, such as binding or gagging, or (*b*) "duress per minas," that is, threats so dreadful and instant as to destroy

the possibility of free choice, or (c) personal ascendency. This last can hardly be admitted as a bar to responsibility in the case of adults who are *compos mentis*, excepting in the form of hypnotic suggestion. The " tyranny of the fixed idea," whether suggested by others or arising from within, certainly destroys the liberty of choice. But as the passive co-operation of the patient is at first necessary, the responsibility is merely transferred further back to the time when the individual originally submitted himself to the ascendency of the hypnotizer or the incendiary orator.

(4) The presence of adequate moral motive in the shape of moral feeling, which is not necessarily implied by the normal development of the intellectual faculties. The moral idiot is incapable of social sympathy or other unselfish impulses.[1]

[1] Havelock Ellis, "The Criminal," pp. 229-231.

CHAPTER IV.

HEDONISTIC THEORIES.

§ 1. The Hedonistic Calculus.

In chapter ii. we have already discussed some of the fundamental points which lie at the basis of any hedonistic theory of ethics. It has been pointed out that pleasure is an abstraction, that we do not commonly desire pleasure, and that if we did this would not prove that pleasure is itself desirable. Let us waive these considerations and consider in detail some of the assumptions made by the scientific hedonists.

Pleasures are commonly regarded as capable of rough quantitative treatment. We speak of one pleasure as being greater than another. The hedonists as a rule try to make this quantitative treatment precise. They assume that there is such a thing as a unit of pleasure, and that units of pleasure can be added, subtracted, and multiplied. Regarded by itself, and without reference to other pleasures and pains which may accompany it, the value (*i.e.*, desirability) of a pleasure depends according to Bentham on its (1) intensity, (2) duration, (3) certainty, and (4) proximity. Proximity resolves itself into certainty, and certainty only affects the estimate of a pleasure not yet present. The two most important circumstances are intensity and duration.

(i.) Bentham and his followers assume that the "intensity of a pleasure can be balanced against its duration." This is indeed commonly believed by the plain man to be possible in a rough way. But if we want to base a scientific theory of morals on it we must be more precise. It implies the notion of a unit of pleasure, which is not a really possible conception. The pleasure of eating an ounce of chocolate is not an invariable quantity, but depends on psychological factors which vary constantly. For instance, the unit of pleasure varies with the antecedent desire; the eagerness of pursuit determines the pleasure of attainment as frequently as the anticipated pleasure of attainment determines the eagerness of pursuit. Setting aside this difficulty in the conception of a unit of pleasure, we note that Bentham and other scientific hedonists assume that if we have x units of pleasure and y units of time $xy = \frac{x}{n} \times ny$ and also $nx \times \frac{y}{n}$, where n is any integer. It does not seem that this is really so. Are five minutes with a certain intensity of pleasure equivalent to an hour with just one-twelfth the same intensity of pleasure; even if we suppose that no disturbing feelings of ennui, etc., enter? Suppose a man has twenty years of life, and is capable of x units of pleasure in each day. Is it a matter of indifference, from a purely hedonistic standpoint, whether he has (disregarding leap years) $20 \times 365 \times x$ units of pleasure in one day, and no pleasure every other day for the rest of his life, that is for $20 \times 365 - 1$ days, or whether he has just x units of pleasure for 20×365 days?

(ii.) That pains must be regarded as negative quantities of pleasure. This again seems open to question. It does not on reflection appear clear that $2x$ units of pleasure $+$ x units of pain $=$ x units of pleasure. A glass of ginger beer unaccompanied by the toothache seems to me out of all proportion pleasanter than a glass of champagne accompanied by ever so mild a twinge while drinking it. Pain appears to have a very real character of its own, and to entirely elude all attempts to take it as merely neutralizing pleasure. And the same thing is true of pleasure: it does not merely neutralize an equivalent amount of pain. x units of pleasure experienced along with x units of pain will be felt as a mixture of pleasure and pain, but with the pain largely preponderating. It will certainly not be felt as a state of neutral excitement.

§ 2. The Commensurability of Pleasures.

(iii.) That all pleasures are commensurable. This supposes that the distinction between true and false, real and unreal pleasures, is invalid. We cannot hold with Plato[1] that there are some pleasures which are in

[1] Cf. "Philebus."

their own nature false because they depend on groundless anticipation of other pleasure. With Protarchus in the "Philebus" we must believe that the falsity lies in the opinion and not in the actual pleasure. Even in the case of "impure" pleasures, pleasures which are mixed with pains, the element of falsity lies in the judgment and not in the pleasure itself. Pleasures exist as they are felt; their intensity is what it appears to be. The judgment passed at the time is the only valid one; and although subsequent experience may show that the pleasure is less than we expected, or that the pleasure is inevitably attended with pain, this reflection does not invalidate the original contemporary judgment that this state is truly and really pleasant.

A more important matter is this, that the hedonistic calculus, Bentham's moral arithmetic, involves the reduction of all qualitative differences in any pleasures into quantitative. It is not open to a consistent hedonist to say with Mill[1] that "it is better to be a human being dissatisfied than a pig satisfied; better to be Socrates dissatisfied than a fool satisfied." We may, as systematic empirical hedonists, hold that "it is quite compatible with the principle of utility [*i.e.*, empirical hedonism] to recognize the fact that some *kinds* of pleasure are more desirable and more valuable than others." But only in so far as the difference of quality can be expressed as a difference of quantity.

We may admit that a unit of pleasure of one kind

[1] Mill, "Utilitarianism," chap. ii.

is not always equal in preferableness to a unit of pleasure of some other kind. But here our units of pleasurableness are different. We must assume that all pleasures can be reduced to one unit. An hour of conscientious satisfaction may be worth many hours of the pleasures of eating; but if we are to estimate one against the other we must suppose them ultimately commensurable—that the former is worth five, ten, or fifty times the latter; and when we have fixed on our equivalent we must not allow any considerations of the supreme dignity of the former (for they have already been taken into account in fixing the equivalent) to prevent our preferring fifty-one hours of eating to only one of conscientious satisfaction. Unless we are willing to weigh pleasures against each other, the whole hedonistic method falls to the ground.[1]

Yet we seem obliged to allow with Mill that " neither pains nor pleasures are homogeneous, and pain is always heterogeneous with pleasure." If this means anything, it means that no system of moral arithmetic is possible. Mill, however, seems to think that though they are in their nature incapable of comparison, yet that we can arrive at valid judgments by appealing to " experience," the fetish of the school to which he belonged. But even experience cannot tell us whether two hours or three bushels is the greater.

There are theoretical difficulties, it may be said, depending on somewhat abstruse psychological conside-

---

[1] Bentham, "Principles of Morals and Legislation," chap. ii., § 4. Sidgwick, "Methods," book ii., chap. ii., § 2.

rations, with regard to which experts themselves are at variance. Even if we admit this objection to be valid there remain obvious *practical* difficulties, some of which are discussed in the next section.

§ 3. Uncertainty of our hedonic judgments.

The next assumption of the hedonistic school is (iv.) That our judgments of the intensity of pleasures can be relied on.

Unfortunately our judgments frequently vary. The same dish tasted when we are hungry and when we are satiated, when ill and when well, will be differently appraised : which judgment is true ? Both, it may be said ; the pleasure is different though the dish is the same. This, however, only comes to the statement that pleasant feeling is as pleasant as at the moment of feeling it is felt to be; which emphasizes the essentially subjective character of pleasure, and suggests that, properly speaking, we can make no assertions at all claiming to be true or false about it. My judgments vary, then, from time to time; and when I reflect on things that pleased me as a boy or a baby, I realize the enormous amount of change which my criterion of pleasure, or my sensibility, has undergone. Yet I cannot say my boyish judgments were wrong. I cannot hold that I was fundamentally deceived in believing that the pleasure of eating toffee was superior to the pleasure of reading Virgil. I am not sure that my present judgments are really superior in accuracy to those I formerly passed; or that those I shall pass in ten years time will be the same as those I pass to-day. Changes of temperament, and sensibility, and purely physiological changes make it impossible for the hedonist to look before and after.

And if we attempt to rectify our judgments by comparison with those of others, we find still greater difficulties. Their opinions, whether expressed individually and personally, or in the collective form of social rules and adages, are notoriously at variance with each other. There is comparatively little disagreement on the broad question that this or that object is pleasure-giving; the difficulty comes in when we want to get precise ideas as to relative pleasurableness. The philosopher, the man of the world, the lover of pleasure, the soldier, the artist and the merchant, the man and the woman, can never agree. Nor can we settle the question in the cavalier manner of Mill, who says that if the fool or the pig is of a different opinion from the philosopher, "it is because they only know their own side of the question. The other party to the comparison knows both sides." Readers of Mill's "Autobiography" will be disposed to doubt whether he himself, with his extraordinary precocity and his eminently ethical temper, would be a fair judge of the pleasures of an active and somewhat irregular life, such as that of a soldier or sailor.

§ 4. Failure of Arithmetical Hedonism.

Dr. Sidgwick admits that scientific hedonism does not rest on an empirical basis; but it would seem that he has neglected to indicate clearly on what other basis it can rest. Some writers, *e.g.*, Mr. Spencer, assume that although perhaps pleasures do not admit of exact measurements, they admit of sufficiently definite estimates to guide conduct. Even if they cannot be arranged in a scale of desirability, some rough approximation can be formed; since we are certainly able to say with tolerable certainty that some pleasures are greater than others, that half a loaf is better than no bread, and that two loaves are better than one. But this will carry us a very little way. To put the matter on this footing is practically to give up hedonism as a system. The tendency to pleasure is no longer our criterion of what is right, and pleasure is no longer our direct aim.

We may indeed trust merely to the deliverances of common sense, the aggregate average judgment of civilized mankind. Such judgment as the organized hedonic experience of society is more likely to be right than my own, or that of the few people I can consult. But if we always trust to this standard, while we are hedonist in accepting pleasure as the supreme good, we are not hedonistic in method; and an identification is little more than a pious opinion of no practical importance. If we venture sometimes to decide differently from common sense we shall do so on quite insufficient grounds, since our own narrow experience, even if supplemented by that of our friends, can never, as we have seen, furnish us with sufficient ground of decision.

§ 5. Egoism and Altruism.

An egoistic view of Ethics recognizes as ultimate only duty to oneself, viz., to seek one's own good. If *good* be taken to mean pleasure and absence of pain, the theory will be what Mr. Sidgwick calls egoistic hedonism. If *good* is not interpreted to mean mere pleasure and absence of pain, the theory, although egoistic, is not hedonistic.

On the other hand, altruism, strictly speaking, should mean *vivre pour autrui*—it is the doctrine of self-sacrifice. A is to care *only* for the happiness of B, C, D, etc. Utilitarianism puts *my* happiness on the same level as that of others; absolute altruism refuses to acknowledge it at all.

Excessive egoism and absolute altruism are alike self-destructive. My happiness depends on the goodwill of those about me. No man is so independent as to be without the need of others; from the moment of birth to the moment of death we are dependent on those about us, or on society at large, for everything that makes life worth having. Besides, few men are so self-centred as to be without the need of seeing others happy, or at any rate free from pain.

This goodwill and this absence of sympathetic pain can only be acquired by living to some extent for others. The practical danger, to most reflective men, rather lies in that refined sort of egoism which refuses to suffer sympathetic pain caused by depriving others of pleasures which are dangerous, or by inflicting pain which is salutary. There is, however, a special theoretical difficulty with regard to egoism as a speculative theory of Ethics.

Suppose I hold that the only right and reasonable end of conduct is my own happiness, and agree that normally my own happiness will be best secured by paying considerable attention to the happiness of others, may I assume that this will always be so and that the two will never be in final and irreconcilable rivalry? Self-sacrifice will not be reasonable, and therefore not right, for me if I find that it is ultimately antagonistic to my own happiness.

Religion steps in here with the rewards of a future life. And if we may go beyond the sphere of mere Ethics and take in theological considerations, these considerations will be of course overwhelming, at least in most cases. But the arguments for the existence of a God who punishes the guilty and rewards the innocent are not regarded as convincing by everyone, especially by those who are most likely to act in a selfish fashion. And theologians have so often taught that the allotment of heaven and hell will be decided by the acceptance or non-acceptance of certain metaphysical or theological beliefs, that even among Christians the ethical effectiveness of the appeal to a future life has been a good deal weakened.

Professor Sidgwick leaves the question unsettled in the last chapter of his "Methods of Ethics." The practical reason, that is, reason exercised on moral matters, seems to give us two conflicting intuitive judgments [1]—one of which asserts that it is reasonable and right to aim at our own happiness and not to ultimately and absolutely give that up for the benefit of anyone else; while the other asserts that we ought to sacrifice our own happiness when we can thereby secure a greater happiness for anyone else. Professor Sidgwick cannot see how these can be reconciled in a way which is entirely convincing to reason.

Most men doubtless make a "venture of faith" here. And in actual practice the importance of the question is slight. In scarcely any cases are the highest interests of self, even when estimated in terms of pleasure and pain, in irreconcilable conflict with those of others.

It is obvious that absolute altruism defeats itself. Self-sacrifice when carried to excess means the enfeeblement or even the destruction of those who practice it, and thus, theoretically speaking, can only lead in the long run to the increased predominance of egoism. This is urged very strongly by Mr. Spencer.[2] But we must not forget that excess of altruism in the few may be in the highest degree useful to society, because the inducements to self-sacrifice are so much

---

[1] This is the Dualism of the Practical Reason. See p. 98, note, below.

[2] Data of Ethics ("Principles of Ethics," Part I.), pp. 196 *seq.*

feebler than the inducements to self-preservation, and, therefore, beautiful and fascinating examples of self-sacrifice are required to overcome the natural antipathy to suffering, and to produce even a quite moderate amount of altruism in ordinary men.

> "The noblest gift a hero leaves his race
> Is to have been a hero."

Mr. Spencer's other contention, that excessive altruism will only lead to the greater selfishness of those who are already selfish, and on whom benefits are heaped, may be dismissed as quite chimerical. The higher altruism understands how to say No.

§ 6. Utilitarianism.

Utilitarianism is defined by Professor Sidgwick as "the ethical theory, that the conduct which, under any given circumstances, is objectively right, is that which will produce the greatest amount of happiness on the whole; that is, taking into account all whose interests are affected by the conduct." In short it is the theory which accepts as the end of conduct "the greatest happiness of the greatest number."

This universalistic hedonism must be distinguished from egoistic hedonism, which regards my own happiness as the only rational end for me. The name, utilitarianism, popularized by J. S. Mill,[1] has been some-

[1] Mill lays claim to being the first to adopt it. See "Utilitarianism," ch. ii., p. 9, note. But Bentham was the real author; see Bowring's note in the "Deontology" (1834), vol. i., p. 287.

times applied to the latter as well as the former. And Bentham himself, as well as Paley and other writers, has used language which shows that he does not always clearly discriminate between them, *e.g.*, " By the principle of utility is meant that principle which approves or disapproves of every action whatsoever, according to the tendency which it appears to have to augment or diminish the happiness of the party *whose interest is in question.*"

We must, therefore, dissociate pure utilitarianism from the crypto-egoism of Hobbes and other writers. The obligation to do what promotes the general happiness according to them rests on the consequences which society attaches to our acts. In a state of nature, *i.e.*, in the imaginary pre-social condition, "the notions of right and wrong, justice and injustice, have no place. Where there is no common power, there is no law; where no law, no injustice." This view comes to much the same thing as that of Thrasymachus in the "Republic"—that justice is the interest of the stronger, for that in all states justice is constituted by the interest of the government.[1]

Utilitarianism makes both the virtuousness and the obligation of a felicific act consequences of its felicific character.

By Bentham, Paley, Mill, and others of what we may call the more orthodox utilitarians, the happiness which is to be sought for each and all as far as

---

[1] Hobbes, "Leviathan," Part I., chap. xiii.; cf. Plato, "Republic," bk. i.

possible, is simply the sum of pleasures. Happiness means pleasure and nothing else. If we reckon pains as negative quantities of pleasures, we may call happiness the algebraical sum of pleasure.

Suppose that we substitute for this meaning of happiness the idea of welfare, goodness, or some other term into which non-hedonistic elements enter, we shall have a hybrid system which is no longer what Bentham propounded, and Mill (though inconsistently) professed.

It will make considerable difference in our results, whether or not we accept the view put forward by Bentham, and accepted by Professor Sidgwick, that all pleasures are homogeneous and commensurable and equally desirable. From this it will follow that "given equal amounts of pleasure pushpin is as good as poetry" (see above § 2). If, on the other hand, we do not analyse the idea of happiness into mere pleasure, or if while doing this we interpret pleasure in an ideal way, we are led to results which coincide with some forms of intuitionism. Thus the late T. H. Green identifies to a large extent the theory of utilitarianism as understood by Mill and George Eliot with his own ethical view. "We can only have the highest happiness .... by having wide thoughts, and much feeling for the rest of the world as well as ourselves; and this sort of happiness often brings so much pain with it, that we can only tell it from pain by its being what we would choose before everything else, because our souls see it is good."[1]

[1] Epilogue to "Romola."

Again, we may admit that all virtuous acts are useful, but deny that utility is the essential and constitutive feature of a virtuous act. This is the position of several of the earlier members of what we may call by prolepsis the utilitarian school. Locke holds that there is a sort of pre-established harmony between virtue and happiness; "God," he tells us, "has by an inseparable connection joined virtue and public happiness together." Smith admits that all moral acts are really useful to ourselves or others, although he does not identify utility with moral quality. It is left for Paley to go a step farther when he not only says that "actions are to be estimated by their tendency to promote happiness," but adds, "it is the utility of any moral rule which alone constitutes the obligation of it."

To the genuine utilitarian rightness is a *proprium* of the useful action; though forming no part of the meaning of the term, it is not only universally present where utility is found, but is an actual consequence of utility.

Finally, we must dissociate from the purely ethical theory called utilitarianism the special psychological opinions which have been held by prominent utilitarians, and which have, therefore, been popularly confounded with it. It is no part of utilitarianism that men always and necessarily desire pleasure: or that they habitually or inevitably choose the greater of two conflicting pleasures. Nor is it *de fide* that the moral concepts, or moral emotions, are derived by association or otherwise from simpler forms; for instance, that conscience is developed in the individual or the race from experience of punishment and reward, or of the natural consequences of conduct.

A utilitarian is not logically bound to teach that A must regard the happiness of B, C, D, X, Y, Z, as his concern in the same way and to the same extent as his own. While A must never sacrifice B's share of happiness in order to secure an equal amount or a less amount for himself, he may yet believe that in general the happiness of each will be best secured by himself. The utilitarian will act usually as an enlightened egoist would do; but he will never deliberately sacrifice the greater pleasure of another to preserve less for himself, and the enlightened egoist will conceive it right to do so. Practically, no doubt, the habit of regard for the welfare of others is likely to be much stronger in the utilitarian than the egoist. The attitude of permanent watchfulness over one's own interest is liable to make the egoist miss many opportunities of sympathetic enjoyment. But (theoretically, at least) this need not necessarily occur.

§ 7. The Proof of Utilitarianism.

What sort of evidence can be offered to prove that the Greatest Happiness of the Greatest Number is the only right end of action? It is a synthetic proposition, and a new predicate is affixed to the subject. It must be provable, if at all, either *a posteriori* or *a priori*.

Mill offered an *a posteriori* proof ("Utilitarianism," chap. iv.). The first part of his argument comes to this. Happiness (*i.e.*, pleasure) is universally desired, and is therefore intrinsically desirable. With this we have already dealt (chap. ii, § 4), and it has been shown that, as a fact, we do not universally desire happiness (*i.e.*, pleasure), and that if we did, it would not prove that happiness is intrinsically desirable. But assuming that Mill has proved his point, what has he proved? That his own happiness is rationally desirable to everybody is not the same thing as that everybody's happiness is rationally desirable to everybody else. Grant that A's happiness is desirable to A, B's to B, and so on. But to prove this is not the same thing as to prove that the happiness of B, C, and so on, is desirable to A as well as his own.

It is to meet this difficulty that Sidgwick advances an *a priori* argument ("Methods," bk. iii., chaps. xiii., xiv). He lays down, in this, perhaps, the most original and important part of his book:—

(1.) That there is an objective right and wrong, independent of my own subjective wants; nothing is right for me which is not right for every one in my circumstances. What is reasonable for me is reasonable for all other men similarly situated. This is Clarke's Rule of Equity.

(2.) That happiness, the greatest possible sum of pleasure, is the reasonable end of action. This he proves by considerations already discussed.

(3.) That my happiness is no more important than

yours, merely because it is mine. Hence that your happiness should be part of my aim. This is Clarke's Rule of Benevolence, though in a new form.[1]

Each of these three steps in the proof is due to an intuition. It cannot be itself proved by further inference, though like other axioms it can be illustrated and explained.

It does not appear that the two former steps need special discussion. The third is the all-important point. Everything depends on this, and it is obviously intended to supply the missing link in Mill's argument. That it sufficiently strengthens the weak point is, I think, very open to question.

Dr. Sidgwick expresses it thus :—" By considering the relation of the integrant parts to the whole and to each other I obtain the self-evident principle that the good of any one individual is of no more importance, from the point (if I may so say) of the Universe, than the good of any other ; unless, that is, there are special grounds for believing that more good is likely to be realized in the one case than in the other." And again, "the good or welfare of any one individual must, as such, be an object of rational aim to any other reasonable individual no less than his own similar good or welfare " (" Methods," bk. iii., chap. xiii., §§ 4, 5). After all this only seems to assert that A's happiness and B's happiness are equally near and important to a third person, C. It does not prove that they are, or ought to be, equally important to A and to B them-

[1] See below, chap. v., § 5.

selves; and in fact Dr. Sidgwick lays down that it is equally intuitive and equally true that our own happiness is the supreme concern of each of us.[1] It is just because we are sentient beings as well as rational that the equal concern for everybody else, which is rational from the universal point of view, is not rational for us. And it seems that if Dr. Sidgwick had for the generic term good substituted the more specific term pleasure, which is actually required for his proof of utilitarianism, this defect in his argument would have been more apparent.

A's happiness and B's happiness are equally near and important to C, but not to either A or B.

Professor Sidgwick's argument seems to fail in just the same way as Mill's. In both of them there lies a fallacy of division. All men taken together reasonably desire the universal happiness of all, but it does not follow that A reasonably desires the happiness of all.

Dr. Sidgwick allows that if the egoist puts his case in this way, I *ought* to aim at my own happiness, there is no absolute way of universalizing his maxim, and showing that his egoism logically implies an equal regard for the happiness of others. But such an inversion of the usual order of thought has not been put forward seriously by any thinker.

It is of course not difficult to show that regard for my own happiness may in nearly every case be practically attained by habitually aiming at that of others.

[1] See below, p. 113, note.

This is a favourite commonplace with eighteenth and early nineteenth century writers.

But it is very difficult to prove that we can best secure our own happiness by habitually regarding the happiness of others as *equally* important to us with our own. In point of fact, as has been said, the utilitarian is obliged to assume that a certain derivative and practical egoism is necessary. And it is quite impossible to prove that the interests of oneself and of others can never clash. It is mere abuse of terms to say that self-sacrifice may be the greatest pleasure. Whatever may be the pleasures of martyrdom, which of late have probably been somewhat overrated, they are always very " impure " (in the Benthamic sense of the word), and usually very evanescent.

Failing the attempted reconciliation put forward by Dr. Sidgwick, we are driven either (1) to accept the ultimate reasonableness of egoism, or (2) to give up hedonism as a complete and independent system. If happiness is the *summum bonum* at all, it must be the happiness of each for each. This conclusion, with which Butler was content,[1] is not in itself so shocking as might be supposed. Practically, it would probably make no great difference in the action of the vast majority of those who are seeking to lead moral and reasonable lives. And although morality would suffer by a lowering of its ideals, and self-sacrifice would

---

[1] See his sermon upon the Love of our Neighbour (XI.), which practically admits that the duty of self-love takes precedence over that of love to others.

lose one of its motives (the conviction that it is reasonable as well as natural), yet some compensation might be found in the promulgation of a short and easy method of being good, a royal road to virtue.

§ 8. Objections to Utilitarianism with regard to Distribution.

We have spoken at length of the difficulties common to all hedonistic methods. There are in the case of utilitarianism special difficulties relating to distribution. Bentham and his school put forward the Greatest Happiness of the Greatest Number as the one ultimate and necessary starting point of ethics. They asserted that a complete ethical system could be built up on it. As a matter of fact the maxim simply declares what is desirable, and requires to be supplemented by further statements, (1) as to the persons who are to be counted in the "number," and (2) as to how we are to divide the pleasure between them.

In the "greatest number" are we to include (1), all our own countrymen; (2), all white men; (3), all civilized persons; (4), all men now alive? Are we to include (5) posterity? And if so, how far in advance is our regard to go? The usual answer is that we are to regard all men, including all posterity, in so far as our action can influence their happiness. But this leaves us in a hopeless difficulty. We cannot tell how far the effects of our action may extend. And we shall somehow find that what benefits our own countrymen or our own age, may be harmful to other men living or to posterity. And as foreigners, or at any rate posterity, will be an infinitely larger total than our own countrymen now alive, we may be driven to the conclusion that we must not regard the interests of the latter. We must not use up our coal for fear posterity may suffer. We must not add to our state debts for the same reason.

The difficulty becomes more if, as modern feeling seems to demand, we include the lower animals in our "greatest number." Anti-vivisectionists already demand that each dog or cat is to count for one, and to declare that remedies purchased at the cost of sufferings to a few scores of rabbits and puppies are in their nature immoral. We must no more cure hydrophobia by Pasteurism than cure skin diseases by bathing in the blood of children, like the sultan in the oriental story. Is every animal to count for one? or shall we have a table of fractions? However small the hedonic fraction assigned, say to herrings, the unbounded consumption of roe will in time extinguish as much happiness as even an epicure is capable of. The extension of the herring fishery, regarded as praiseworthy at Yarmouth, becomes a criminal matter when viewed from the point of view of the herring or the vegetarian.

On what principle are we to distribute a given amount of pleasure? Bentham lays down that "everybody is to count for one, and nobody for more than one;" and this principle has apparently been accepted by all utilitarians. It cannot be evolved from the axiom that the Greatest Happiness of the Greatest Number is the ultimate aim of all virtuous action. It is a new axiom, and involves the assumption of an extrinsic standard of justice; in other words, its adoption is a tacit confession that we cannot bring all virtues under the Greatest Happiness formula.

But what does the new axiom mean? It seems to assume that all men have the same capacity for pleasure and pain. This is notoriously untrue. There are certain kinds of enjoyment for which most men have very little or no capacity. The pleasures of art and of the pursuit of truth are confined to a small fraction of the civilized races. How many millions of people in the world derive any appreciable pleasure from hearing the best music or seeing the best pictures? We cannot distribute equal amounts of this sort of pleasure to a refined and educated man, the average artizan, and the average Kaffir, any more than we can distribute equal amounts of light to a clear-sighted person, a patient with cataract, and a blind man. The only rational plan will be to exclude the incapable from the distribution. To put it in another way. Some men have a greater quantitative capacity for pleasure than others. Suppose we have $4x$ units of pleasure to give away, and that Prospero's capacity is denoted by $3x$, Caliban's by x. If we give $2x$ units to each, Caliban will simply waste x units; while Prospero will be still far from completely happy. Surely it will be better to give Prospero $3x$ and Caliban x. And as the capacity for pleasure varies, it would seem that, if we are to aim at the production of as much pleasure as possible, we ought to take in hand chiefly those persons who are most capable of happiness, otherwise our trouble will be to some extent wasted.

The truth is, men are no more equal in their capacity for enjoyment than in anything else. And the axiom will have to be accepted in a very special and non-natural way, if it is to be accepted at all. All are to count for one, unless we can show cause against it. The presumption is to be in favour of equality. But this equality is only in the abstract; when we come to concrete facts we shall have to acknowledge that the pleasure of a bushman is not equally desirable with that of a bishop, quantitatively as well as qualitatively.

But we are entirely without guidance as to what will be the ratio between them. Instead of the delightful simplicity of "each to count for one," we are likely to find ourselves requiring an elaborate schedule of hedonic constants.

A further difficulty of distribution arises, when we remember that "Greatest Happiness of the Greatest Number" may mean greatest total happiness or greatest average happiness. If the former, the end of universalistic hedonism will be to increase population as much as possible. No matter how small the pleasure in the lot of the individual, as long as any pleasure is left at all, we can make the aggregate sum of pleasure indefinitely great by increasing the number of persons who possess it. If, as seems more reasonable, the happiness of the average individual is regarded, a restricted population, each member of which is in possession of considerable sources of pleasure, will be our aim.

§ 9. The Vagueness of Utilitarianism.

The earlier utilitarians, such as Paley and Bentham, regarded its superior clearness as one of the chief claims of their theory to the acceptance of practical people. Morality became almost a matter of demonstration. And even the chastened enthusiasm of Dr. Sidgwick regards utilitarianism as a clearer and more practical system than the intuitional morality which it was put forward to supplant.[1]

Indeed, one of the most effective arguments put forward by Professor Sidgwick is the cumulative proof that ordinary common sense morality is vague and uncertain, and that it naturally turns to utilitarianism to help it out.

We may ask to begin with, Why is it necessary that morality should be precise? Other arts besides the art of conduct are content to put up with a certain amount of uncertainty, *e.g.*, politics, and the fine arts.[2]

It is only on the jural view of ethics, which throws all ethical principles into the form of rules,

---

[1] There are, as we have just seen (p. 75), some Hedonists who do not regard pleasure as measurable, and reject the moral arithmetic of Bentham.

[2] Cf. Aristotle, "Nic. Eth.," book i., chap. iii.

that the demand for precision arises. And it is open to question whether the highest kind of morality is compatible with ethical codification. Spontaneous impulse which has an important place in virtuous conduct does not easily admit of legal precision.

Then again, if we are to have rules, whatever these rules may be, we shall find much the same difficulty in bringing cases under them which common sense morality finds. Utilitarians have nearly the same difficulty in applying their maxims as other moralists have in applying their less pretentious ones. The casuistry of consequences is as difficult as any other casuistry.

Suppose I am in doubt as to some act, *e.g.*, some deviation from veracity. I may consider the act proper to be done, because if the exact circumstances under which I am placed be taken into account, I should really desire all persons in like circumstances to act in the same way. But I may consider it not proper to be done, because my exact circumstances would never really be taken into account, men would do the act in less exceptional cases, and their love of veracity would get weakened. Which of these two considerations shall be regarded as preponderant will depend on the distance to which we trace the tendency of the act. There may be a clear gain of pleasure to myself in unveracity; and yet the second consideration may lead me to hesitate, for the real though less marked influence for evil on those who know me, and their example on others, may outweigh the benefit to myself. Still, this influence on others, though at first disastrous, may eventuate in the rules as to veracity being altered, so that more accurate distinctions may be introduced, and the act which I actually did, and which I believe to be legitimate, viz., speaking an untruth under certain special circumstances, may be definitely permitted. This seems a clear gain; but reflection may show that such an alteration may tend to a general enfeeblement of morality, because every set of exceptions tends to weaken the influence of those main rules on which after all the fabric depends. Now each of these considerations applies to a greater number of persons than the preceding.

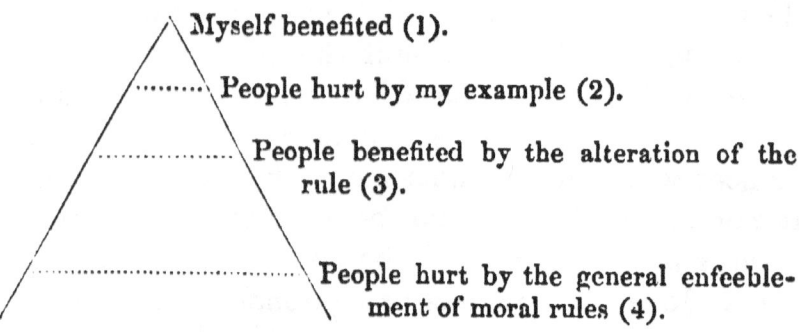

Each person is affected less, but it is quite possible that the increase in *extension* may much more than compensate for decrease in *intension*. We may stop at the level we have reached, practically assuming (as many conservative utilitarians do) that it can never be right to do anything which can possibly be misinterpreted by anybody, and that therefore it can never be right to try to alter rules of conduct at all. But we might go a step further, and urge (as many radical utilitarians do) that this weakening of positive conventional morality will eventuate in a higher and more enlightened morality avowedly based on utility; and this benefit affecting every member of society will absolutely outweigh all the disadvantages attending it.

This sort of see-saw, it may be said, is inevitable in all moral reasoning. But the chief point to be noticed is that the process is not mere see-saw ; it lands us in one or other of two conclusions, one of which will justify *no* infringement of a rule, while the other will justify *any* infringement of a rule, and gives us no help to decide between them.

This it seems is the logical outcome of a method which professes to give results of a specially definite and practical kind.

§ 10. Evolutionary Hedonism.

At the end of chapter i. we saw that some thinkers regard the standard or criterion of good conduct to lie in conduciveness to the welfare of society; but that they assume that this will mean in the long run the happiness of all. For the supporters of this view pleasure is still the ultimate end; they are hedonists, but with a difference. They hold that pleasure for all must not be made the direct object of conduct. Our direct object should be the welfare of society, the increase of life of the organism in which we are, so to speak, biological units or cells; and this will carry with it, at any rate when sufficiently advanced, increase of life for each, involving increase of happiness.

One objection to this theory lies in the assumption that the increased life of the whole involves increased life of the parts. In the development of an organic form, many cells, tissues, or organs (our biological metaphors are perhaps a little vague) must be degraded, or destroyed, in order that the development of the whole may take place. The most successful societies (*quâ* societies) that history tells us of are societies in which the individual consciousness has been most repressed by the forces of solidarity. The necessary economising of energy by habit and custom tends to the suppression of consciousness both in the individual and the society. The complete adaptation of society to its environment, carrying with it the complete adaptation of the individual to his, would mean, if we suppose it possible, the suppression of the higher forms of consciousness, reason, and will.

Such a complete adaptation is, however, unthinkable. Nor need the evolutionist necessarily assume it, if he posits social health as the end for each and all, irrespective of the pleasure which may or may not accompany it. But then he is left with no means of showing that such social welfare is desirable. He merely shows that it occurs. Desirable must mean desirable for some one.

Mr. Spencer and Mr. Leslie Stephen reject the moral arithmetic of Bentham and the orthodox utilitarians as unsatisfactory. Mr. Leslie Stephen, for instance, lays stress on the unscientific character of utilitarianism. It overlooks the fact that, because society is an organism, you cannot consider any individual action by itself. The real consequences of an action " can only be traced when we recognize the nature of the Social structure, which again implies the existence of a certain stage of individual development, and neither of these is deducible from the properties of the assumed unit," viz., the normal human being of to-day. "Human nature is not constant, but, on the contrary, a variable, and the aim of the moralist is precisely to modify it." The utilitarian objects to, say, murder, "because in the existing state of society it does more harm than good. But suppose we get rid of some of the feelings concerned" (apparently such as foolish pity for the victim, or excessive dislike of disorder) " might we not be the happier on the whole?" To answer this, the utilitarian has to "compare the amount of happiness in two societies agreeing only in the circumstance that both are composed of men, which seems to render the whole problem too intricate and indeterminate for practical application."[1]

At the same time the utilitarian calculus will be of service in determining what we shall do here and now. "The actual progress in morality is always determined at every point by utilitarian considerations. But when we try to generalize from this and

[1] Leslie Stephen, "Science of Ethics," pp. 363 *seq.*

to say that the form of morality, or the criterion of moral conduct, is the tendency to produce happiness, we get into difficulties. The reason is that already given. We are generalizing in such a way as to omit an essential condition of an accurate statement. We are taking constants for variables, and variables for constants."[1]

As new moral instincts are acquired, the individual changes and the structure of society changes. The happiness of the individual in the new stage of development differs in degrees and (apparently) in kind from that of the individual in whom these instincts do not exist. "The moral instincts of the society correspond ... to the social development, and express at every instant the judgment formed of the happiness and misery caused by corresponding modes of conduct. As they become organized the whole society becomes more efficiently constituted, and its standard of happiness is also modified.... But since the happiness itself changes as the society develops we cannot compare the two societies at different stages as if they were more or less efficient machines for obtaining an identical product."[2]

This criticism of utilitarianism seems a little too academic. It admits that "men actually reason and *are justified in reasoning* provisionally as to moral questions" by the hedonistic calculus. But it denies that such reasoning is scientifically exact, since we can know little of the conditions of happiness which

[1] "Science of Ethics," p. 369. [2] *Ibid.*, p. 370.

obtain in other stages of civilization than our own; which is what all modern utilitarians are perfectly ready to admit.

The conceptions of well-being of society, fuller life of society, and so on, seem to be too vague and indeterminate to afford any definite criteria. After an immense parade of scientific precision the practical outcome of the new teaching is little other that that of a conservative utilitarianism:—Never break a received moral rule, but in doubtful cases, where the rule is uncertain, fall back on moral arithmetic.

CHAPTER V.

INTUITIONIST THEORIES.

§ 1. The word Intuition.

The word intuition has been a source of constant bewilderment to students, and a few words of explanation may well be given to it.

If a traveller sees a building of a certain kind in a place where his map tells him Ely Cathedral stands, and recognizes the building as Ely Cathedral, here there is clearly a process of conscious inference. If next day he sees the same building, and again recognizes it as Ely Cathedral, although the recognition is now practically instantaneous, there is still present an element of inference. The inference is unconscious; it takes the form of a spontaneous synthesis not requiring a special concentration of attention. But it is there. Our perceptions are not, as they appear to be, immediate knowledge; psychological analysis shows that they are in a high degree complex and inferential. To recognize a colour involves unconscious inference; all localization of sensations involves unconscious inference. These inferences, however, must have a starting-point. This ultimate datum which gives occasion for the activity of the mind must be known by an act of immediate cognition. If we subtract all the representative elements in the percept we shall come to something which is immediately presented; whose presentation is the cause of the presence of the representative elements. It may be conceded that such a purely presentative element is never known as such; we only infer its existence. It is, as Dr. Ward says, a "psychological myth." But we have to assume that it exists.

The words "intuition" and "inference," however, are not always used so strictly. Conscious inference differs so much from the unconscious inference, or classification of ideas, which occurs in perception, that we sometimes find writers declining to call them both by the same name. Inference with them means only fully conscious inference. And the word intuition is often used to denote the whole process of perception; we are said to intuite an object, because the representative or inferential factors in the process are unconscious. And by a further extension, we are said to form certain judgments intuitively because we are not conscious of the train of inference which led to them.

Ordinary judgments of perception belong to this class. As a matter of fact such judgments, though involving no process of *conscious* inference, are in a high degree inferential. Other judgments are called intuitive because we cannot assign an inferential origin to them. Such, for instance, are some of the axioms of mathematics, and of physics. We are obliged to assume some truths as ultimate, because we want for our reasonings starting-points which shall be independent of reasoning.[1] Such independent truths we call intuitive. Their validity is guaranteed by merely looking at them, by simple inspection. We know that two straight lines cannot enclose a space, and that every event must have a cause, without experience and without deduction. And it is further guaranteed by the agreement of the results deduced from them with our general experience.

§ 2. Relation between Intuitionism and Hedonism.

It is now obvious that the ordinary and convenient distinction between intuitionism and hedonism is not a perfectly logical one. There are two *fundamenta divisionis*. The intuitionist, as such, is simply committed to the view that the ultimate standards or criteria of conduct cannot be guaranteed by any process of inference, and must therefore rest on intuitions. The hedonist, as such, merely asserts that pleasure is the ultimate good. But the hedonist may have arrived at this result by intuition; may be able to reach it in no other way.

The antithesis, however, is not without justification.

With the average intuitionist the important fact is not what he discovers by intuition, for his results are

[1] Sully, "Outlines of Psychology," p. 283; "Human Mind," vol. i., p. 458.

usually in close agreement with common sense morality; but how he reaches them. For on this *how* he usually bases their claim. His principles commend themselves to general acceptance; what he has to do is to theoretically justify their acceptance. On the other hand, the hedonist is advancing a new basis of morality more or less at variance with common sense: and naturally dwells more on the principle itself, showing its meaning, its limitations, its results, than on the process by which he arrived at it. The content of the principle is the matter of chief importance with him; and in nine cases out of ten he does not know by what logical method it can be adequately demonstrated.

The student must then remember that some intuitionists may be hedonists, and that some hedonists may be intuitionists. He must remember that some intuitionists are deductive and some inductive in their methods; and so with non-intuitionists, if indeed we can assume that any method which entirely excludes an intuitional starting-point is possible.

§ 3. Intuitionism.

We have already explained what is usually meant by intuitionism. The name is given to any theory which assumes that there are certain ethical propositions of a more or less general character, the truth of which is perceived on mere inspection, without any process of reasoning, or which assumes that the rightness of action is a quality which exists in it without reference to any end, and may be immediately cognized. An action is known to be right because it is shown to come under one of these rules of conduct, or because its rightness is immediately apprehended; and not because it tends to the realization of some end. Hence intuitionism is called an *independent* theory of ethics; while hedonism, with which it is usually contrasted, is described as a *dependent* theory. However, there are several theories which, while not hedonistic, are certainly dependent. These are often called intuitionalist, though without adequate reason, since they do not regard the goodness of the action as inherent to the action itself, nor do they accept a number of ethical principles as self-evident, like the axioms of mathematics.

As Professor Sidgwick says, intuitionists are divided as to—

(1) What it is that is intuitively apprehended.

(2) The reason for doing what is intuitively ascertained to be right.

To begin with the former ground of distinction:— There are intuitionists who hold the "ultra-empirical" view. They regard morality as resting on quasi-percepts, or immediate judgments of right and wrong; which are indeed occasionally liable to mistakes— though this is not allowed by every one—but can only be corrected by an appeal to the same faculty of immediate knowledge. These judgments, according to popular opinion, refer to the quality of *actions*;

but Dr. Martineau has developed a variety of the theory which makes them refer to the quality of *motives*.[1]

This doctrine of immediate apprehension of moral qualities naturally gives rise to the moral sense doctrine in its crudest form—viz., that there exists a special faculty which apprehends moral quality as the nose apprehends smells, and with just as little concurrence of reason.

§ 4. Dogmatic Intuitionism.

The doctrine that what we intuitively perceive is the truth of general moral principles, or the rightness of rules of conduct, has been the favourite one with theologians and moralists. We do not immediately recognize a given action as wrong in itself; what we perceive immediately is the wrongness of stealing in general, and not until we can bring the given act under the term stealing do we recognize the act as wrong. The quality of wrongness is in the act all

---

[1] No act is right in itself or wrong in itself. What constitutes the moral character of an act is the motive which stimulates us to perform it. There is a hierarchy of motive impulses, and the relative positions of the different members of it is known infallibly by the conscience. Men inevitably arrive at the same estimate of its value or height of motives. "Every action is *right* which in the presence of a lower motive follows a higher; every action is wrong which in the presence of a higher principle follows a lower." See Martineau, "Types of Ethical Theory," vol. ii., pp. 17-282; Sidgwick, "Methods," bk. iii., chap. xii.

the time; but we do not intuite it, we only infer its existence.

What then are the ultimate principles which are intuitively recognized? There is considerable difficulty in arriving at any definite statement. Allusion is constantly made to such principles in conversation, in serious and informal treatises, but they are seldom cited for inspection. There is no acknowledged table of ethical axioms to which one can appeal. For instance, the ten commandments are obviously something more and something less than such a list. They contain truths or rules which are theological rather than ethical, and which are clearly not intuitive. They need expansion and generalisation; for instance, all theologians are agreed that mere abstention from murder and from adultery does not cover all that is meant by commandments six and seven. Nothing can, of course, be called an ultimate moral principle which is capable of having a reason given for it; but even if we do not insist very rigidly on this condition, there is a difficulty in finding any agreement. That we are not to take the property of others by force or fraud, that we are not to injure their person, that we are not to take away their life, and that we must not take away our own life,—such are among the rules generally put forward as ultimate.

Reid, who may be taken to represent ethical orthodoxy, gives an extended list of " some of the first principles of morals."

A. Relating to " virtue in general " :—

"1. There are some things in human conduct that merit approbation and praise, others that merit blame and punishment; and different degrees either of approbation or of blame, are due to different actions.

"2. What is in no degree voluntary can neither deserve moral approbation nor blame.

"3. What is done from unavoidable necessity may be agreeable or disagreeable, useful or hurtful, but cannot be the object either of blame or of moral approbation.

"4. Men may be highly culpable in omitting what they ought to have done, as well as in doing what they ought not.

"5. We ought to use the best means we can to be well informed of our duty.

"6. It ought to be our most serious concern to do our duty as far as we know it, and to fortify our minds against every temptation to deviate from it."

B. Relating to "particular branches of virtue:"—

"1. We ought to prefer a greater good, though more distant, to a less; and a less evil to a greater.

"2. As far as the intention of nature appears in the constitution of man, we ought to comply with that intention, and to act agreeably to it.

"3. No man is born for himself only.

"4. In every case we ought to act that part towards another which we would judge to be right in him to act toward us, if we were in his circumstances and he in ours.

"5. To every man who believes the existence, the perfection, and the providence of God, the veneration and submission we owe to him is self-evident." (Works, ed. Hamilton, pp. 637-640.)

C. There is a third class which expresses the relations existing between different kinds of good conduct: or to use Reid's own words: "There is another class of axioms in morals by which, when there seems to be an *opposition* between the actions that different virtues lead to, we determine to which the *preference* is due." Such are the following:

(a) "Unmerited generosity should yield to gratitude, and both to justice."

(b) "Unmerited beneficence to those who are at ease should yield to compassion to the miserable, and external acts of piety to works of mercy" (pp. 635-640).

It is characteristic of Reid's want of consistency that this last axiom, or first principle, which he expressly tells us is self-evident, should be (in the very same sentence) deduced from another still more ultimate principle:—"Because God loves mercy better than sacrifice."

This dogmatic intuitionism is essentially unphilosophical. The thinker naturally attempts to systematize and analyze; to reduce his number of principles to the fewest possible, and to exhibit the whole in a connected form. Accordingly, we can scarcely point to any philosopher who has rested content with the system which seems natural enough to the unreflective morality of common sense.[1] The preacher and the teacher, whose aim is practical, are the natural upholders of dogmatic intuitionism.

We may state in the words of Locke the essential point of what is called—

§ 5. Philosophic Intuitionism.

"The idea of a supreme being, infinite in power, goodness, and wisdom, whose workmanship we are, and on whom we depend; and the idea of ourselves as understanding, rational beings, being such as are clear in us, would, I suppose, if duly considered and pursued, afford such foundations of our duty and rules of action as might place morality among the sciences capable of demonstration: wherein, I doubt not, that from self-evident propositions, by necessary consequences as incontestable as those in mathematics, the measures of right and wrong might be made out, to anyone that will apply himself with the same indifferency and attention to the one as he does to the other of these sciences." (Essay, bk. iv., chap. iii., § 18.)

This statement clearly places ethics on the foundation of theology; and Dr. Clarke lays down the main positions of his system in close connection with certain theological propositions:—

"The same necessary and eternal *different relations* that different things bear to one another; and the same

---

[1] Even Reid's discussion shows the beginning of such an attempt.

consequent *fitness* or *unfitness* of the application of different things or different relations one to another; with regard to which the will of God always and necessarily *does* determine itself, to choose to act only what is agreeable to justice, equity, goodness, and truth, in order to the welfare of the whole universe; *ought* likewise constantly to determine the wills of all subordinate rational beings to govern all their actions by the same rules, for the good of the public in their respective stations. That is, these eternal and necessary differences of things make it *fit and reasonable* for creatures so to act; they cause it to be their *duty* or lay an *obligation* upon them so to do, even separate from the consideration of these rules being the *positive will* or *command of God;* and also antecedent to any respect or regard, expectation or apprehension of any *particular private and personal advantage or disadvantage, reward or punishment,* either present or future; annexed either by natural consequence, or by positive appointment, to the practising or neglecting of those rules." (Boyle Lectures, 1705, p. 176, 9th edition.) In other words, there are between things certain ultimate relations existing; amongst them are certain relations we call moral, and these moral relations subsist apart from the direct command of God, in consequence of the existence of the objects of thought themselves. As examples of such ultimate and unalterable relations Clarke cites several theological propositions; *e.g.*, " that God is infinitely superior to men," and " that men should honour, worship, obey, and imitate God;" and several ethical ones, *e.g.*, "that all men should endeavour to promote the universal good and welfare of all." From the apprehension of these truths follow corresponding obligations.

(1.) "That we must honour and worship God."

(2.) "That we so deal with every man as in like circumstances we could reasonably expect he should deal with us" (Rule of equity); and "that we endeavour by a universal benevolence to promote the welfare and happiness of all men" (Rule of love).

(3.) "That every man preserve his own being as long as he is able, and take care to keep himself at all times in such temper and disposition both of body and mind as may best fit him to perform his duty." From this rule of sobriety flow the duties of temperance, self-restraint, contentment, and (apparently) courage and prudence, though Clarke does not explicitly mention them (p. 209).

Putting aside his rule of piety, as belonging to the sphere of religion rather than that of morality, we note that the third rule—that of sobriety—involves a reference to duty as determined independently of it; the third rule is dependent on the second. Professor Sidgwick regards the first branch of the second rule, viz., that of equity, as equivalent to the statement (so far as altruistic action goes) that "if we assert any action to be right, we imply that it would be right for all persons in precisely similar circumstances;" that is, to an assertion of the objectivity of morality.

This axiom, says Dr. Sidgwick, is implied in all

moral reasoning; for this involves the assumption that all ethical principles which are valid at all are ultimately reconcilable ; or perhaps we may say that the moral system is a continuum from any part of which we can pass to any other. It has all the certainty and the self-evidence of a mathematical axiom ("Methods," bk. iii., chap. xiii., § 4).

"Do to others as you would they should do to you" is a practical rule which partly covers this, but also includes other elements ; it suggests to us that gentleness and kindness are, as a fact, likely to produce gentleness and kindness in return, and it therefore does not exclude the immoral possibility that I may assist wicked people in evil in order that they may assist me in some improper enterprise of my own.

The rule of love, as Clarke states it, can hardly be considered as axiomatic. On the face of it it does not seem self-evident that I ought to aim at the good and welfare of all men. And in point of fact Clarke exhibits the evidence for the rule in the following series of propositions :—

"If there be a natural and necessary difference between good and evil; and that which is good is fit and reasonable, and that which is evil is unreasonable, to be done: and that which is the greatest good is always the most fit and reasonable to be chosen: then as the goodness of God extends itself universally over all His works through the whole creation by doing always what is absolutely best in the whole: so every rational creature ought to do all the good it can to its fellow-creatures; to which end universal love and benevolence is plainly the most certain, direct, and effectual means." The first part of this assures the existence of a *summum bonum*, a something which it is intrinsically reasonable to desire for ourselves. The next part makes a theological assumption, and on this apparently rests the obligation of universal beneficence. The third part asserts that universal love and benevolence is the most certain means of fulfilling this obligation. Professor Sidgwick, however, regards (with the slight condition affixed) this rule of love as axiomatic, and paraphrases it thus: "The good of any individual cannot be *more* intrinsically desirable *because it is his*, than the equal good of any other individual." ("Methods," p. 360, 1st edition.) While this last statement may be admitted as axiomatic, it is difficult to regard it as equivalent to Clarke's.

At any rate, his intuitive acceptance of these two propositions, (1) that what is right for one is right for any other, (2) that what is desirable for one is desirable for all, together with certain others, viz., that pleasure is the *summum bonum*, justifies us in placing Dr. Sidgwick amongst the intuitionalists.[1] This does

---

[1] Dr. Sidgwick in other places lays down two propositions as intuitively and finally certain, viz. (1) that it is irrational to sacrifice any part of my own happiness unless I myself gain an equivalent amount of happiness, and (2) that it is rational to sacrifice my own happiness if some one else gains an equivalent increase of happiness. These two propositions constitute together what he has called the "Dualism of Practical Reason." Cf. "Mind," 1889, p. 483; 4th edit. of "Methods," pp. 504 *seq.*

I

not, as has been explained, prevent his being a utilitarian, since there is no real antithesis between intuitionism and hedonism. He is *formally* an intuitionist, and *materially* a utilitarian.

Kant may also be assigned to the group of philosophic intuitionalists, since he builds his system of ethics on certain axioms:—

(1.) That there is an absolute end prescribed by reason to each, which can be arrived at by excluding all empirical and limited ends.

(2.) That this end is reason itself; or, in other words, all rational beings are as such ends to each.

(3.) That the ends aimed at by these rational beings become therefore ends for me as well.

But the attempt to classify a thinker so much *sui generis* as Kant is always more or less unsatisfactory.

§ 6. Objections to Intuitionism.

Against all intuitional doctrines has been advanced the objection that the moral principles held by men differ very widely. Whether these principles are gathered by induction from the approval bestowed on particular acts, or profess to be moral axioms, they are found, it is said, unlike the principles of science, to vary from age to age, and from one state of civilization to another. In Sparta, to cite the *locus classicus*, stealing was held to be laudable; while murder and cruelty are matters of moral obligation in Dahomey. How then, it is asked, can men be said to have immediate perception of right and wrong? We do not find that in any countries or in any ages men have asserted that two straight lines will enclose a space, nor have they ever set about acting as if such a thing were possible.

Reflection seems to show that these differences arise rather in the application of moral principles than in the principles themselves. Thieving is never really substituted for honesty as worthy of moral approval, nor cruelty for mercy. No race has yet been found which has substituted "Thou shalt steal" and "Thou shalt murder" for the commandments as we accept them. Thus the moral intuitions of savages are the same as ours, but their powers of reasoning are less. They do not recognize as stealing or as cruelty what we recognize as such, because they have not yet brought the acts we disapprove under the general principle. Their error lies in the minor premise of the ethical syllogism, not in the major.

It is not difficult to see why such errors arise. We are not governed solely by reason; the savage is scarcely governed at all by reason. All of us are apt to follow the opinions of the society, or even the club or the clique to which we belong; and it seldom happens that these current ideas are submitted to investigation and correction. And, as we shall see later on, feelings of moral approval and disapproval attach themselves as readily and as firmly to a false ethical judgment as to a true one.

It is not sufficiently recognized that one may hold

that the mind perceives the quality of a moral act, or disposition, immediately, and yet believe that the power of perception developes. In psychology we no longer maintain the antithesis between absolute intuitionism and absolute empiricism. Space-knowledge, for instance, comes inevitably to the individual, and it comes in a certain necessary form; it is not an accidental experience which we may have or may not have, as the case may be; yet though some space reference is implied in our earliest definite perceptions, our space knowledge gradually developes. So, too, with our knowledge of self, the empirical ego of the psychologists. And the recognition of the beautiful is at once innate and empirical; our maturer judgments are not contradictions, but expansions, of the crude likings of childhood.

Some writers have indeed gone so far as to assert that the lowest races of men have no moral perceptions at all. Even if this were so, it would not disprove the opinion that civilized men have moral intuitions, and that these intuitions are valid, any more than the fact that some African races cannot count above five implies that Europeans have no recognition of necessary truths in mathematics. The late development of our geometrical and arithmetical perceptions is acknowledged, yet their validity cannot be called into question. In point of fact, however, the most careful observers hold that there is no tribe without moral ideals. Mr. Tylor, for instance, affirms that " the asserted existence of savages so low as to have no moral standard, is too groundless to be discussed." [1]

Be it observed that to admit the existence of moral intuitions does not commit us to any particular view as to the exact nature of the faculty to which they are due. That they are to some extent intellectual products must be granted; but we are under no necessity to assume the existence of "innate ideas," nor even the existence of a special faculty of moral perception. Great confusion has been brought about by the confusion of the terms "innate" and "intuitive," which have really nothing in common. The old doctrine of innate ideas combatted by Locke no longer exists, if, indeed, it ever existed. In some sense, every faculty of mind and body is innate. The ability to respond in a specific way to certain stimuli is born with a man, is a part of his ultimate constitution. But this ability is capable of development or suppression. If the proper stimuli are not applied, the innate faculty will never show itself. Practice, and indeed education, are necessary to teach us even to walk and to speak; but practice and education would produce no effect if the innate capacity were not there.

§ 7. Other so-called Intuitionist theories.

There are other theories, as we have said, which are usually called intuitional, but which present wide

[1] See also Tylor, "Anthropology" (1892), p. 4C7. But compare Lubbock, "Prehistoric Times," pp. 565-6.

divergencies from the foregoing. It is unfortunate that owing to the mistaken antithesis between hedonism and intuitionism all theories which do not easily fit into the former are referred to the latter. The typical intuitional theory is one which lays down certain moral propositions as self-evident, proceeds to deduce other moral principles from them, and determines the obligation of an act by reference to these *axiomata media* or to the ultimate principles. There is almost necessarily a jural or legalistic character in such a system.[1] And on the other hand, a system which does not exhibit this jural character is scarcely ever as intuitional in the strict sense. It seldom aims at exhibiting its principles in the shape of formal propositions. It proclaims conformity to an ideal rather than conformity to a law. Such an ideal cannot be defined; in fact, it is of the essence of an ideal that it is incapable of exact definition. Yet the ideal is concrete, in some sense pictorial. It appeals to and fills the imagination; and thus rouses emotions more powerful than those which accompany the apprehension of an axiom or a formula.

Perhaps the idealist system, if it can be so called, which can most easily be brought under the general definition of intuition is that of the Stoic *vivere convenienter Naturæ*.

---

[1] Its prescriptions are binding of themselves and for themselves, apart from any end which they help to secure.

§ 8. Life according to Nature.

The Stoics developed the idea of harmony and order, which was always one of the guiding notions in Greek ethical thought, by asking the question, what is to be the standard in accordance with which life is to be ordered? It was Zeno, or one of his immediate disciples, who replied that the regulative standard is nature. The virtuous life is conformed to nature—the universe as an ordered whole, which exhibits in its totality and in its smallest details the Divine Reason which is its formative element. Their philosophy was thus pantheistic. They taught that our activity can only be harmonious and free from discord when it is in agreement with the whole scheme of which we form part. By conforming ourselves to the Reason which directs the universe we shall avoid the errors of our limited intelligence and of our rebellious impulses. But after all, humanity is from most points of view not only a, but the, most important fact in the world. Man's constitution manifests the reasonable order of the universe more distinctly than does anything else. Thus the formula of life according to nature was made more pointed by specific mention of human nature, in addition to, or even apart from the wider expression. Agreement with the true nature of man was the test of right conduct. Virtue consisted in a constant activity in conformity with our own true nature, and entire and vital obedience towards the law of our own being.

This doctrine, though in itself obviously vague and incomplete, has, perhaps, excited more influence on the practical morality of men than any other that has come from the workshop of the philosopher. In two distinct directions has its influence been felt. Grafted on Hebraic theological ideas it was a most important factor in Christian ethics; grafted on Roman legal ideas it became the origin of that broad philosophical study of the law which has been the basis of modern theories of free government. The whole Catholic ascetic theory, with its emphasis on self-restraint and self-abnegation, patience and purity, is leavened with Stoicism; and on this is built mediæval monasticism. On the other hand, the labours of seventeenth and eighteenth century writers on jurisprudence and politics have given us not only our system of international law but also the doctrines of liberalism and individualism.

In a certain sense all our impulses, actions and thoughts are equally natural. They all belong to us, and are alike the outcome of our own nature. In this sense the precept that we should live according to nature is unnecessary and absurd. There is, however, another sense in which it is ordinarily used. Those impulses which are most normal and ordinary, and therefore strongest and most preponderant, are natural in a more definite way than the others. To follow one's strongest impulses is not a very prudent direction; and on examination we find that some of the strongest and most persistent motives are those to which the moralist is least willing to entrust the general direction of our activities. Selfishnesss and lust and passion are among them. Let us see if we can define Nature in a way which will make the Stoic formula less open to criticism. By man's true or real nature we often, perhaps generally, mean not those elements which are strongest but those which are highest, those which most distinguish him from the brute. It lies in no mere impulse, however beautiful; tenderness to offspring and courage we share with the lower animals. It lies in the possession of reason whereby we not only know what is true, but can consciously direct our conduct. Reason is "in nature and in kind" the superior of all other faculties; "to preside and govern from the very economy and constitution of man belongs to it." Appetites, desires and passions may prevail and may imperiously silence the claim to supremacy; but in the moment of pause we acknowledge that such prevalence is " mere usurpation" and "a breaking in upon, and violation of the constitution of man."[1]

We thus come back to an attempt to base ethics on psychology—fortified by the intuition, for which no external evidence can be given, that reason ought to be obeyed. Practically this is the position both of Butler and Kant.

But this process of analysis weakens the impulsive energy of the old ideal of life according to Nature. Its moral force lay in its concreteness; and this was

[1] Butler, "Sermons on Human Nature."

almost destroyed by the substitution of pure reason for the image of the perfectly wise and good man who was the equal of Zeus, and the superior of all terrestrial beings, who lived a life in strange contrast to the artificial and conventional life of the Roman world. Nor has the theistic element in the system as presented by Butler sufficed to atone for the change.

§ 9. Perfectionism.

The essential feature of Perfectionism, as taught by the late T. H. Green and his disciples, is that it makes the *summum bonum* not a definite object or condition which can be gained and possessed, but an ideal well-being which is never absolutely achievable, though capable of nearer and nearer approximation.[1] We cannot assert that any one kind of activity or state of existence is ultimately good. What we mean by good is something more than our ancestors meant by it, something less than our posterity will mean by it. We have all used the concept of good, but its content has become fuller, and in some respects different, with the progress of ages. Even within the limits of individual experience a development something like this takes place. The idea of good, originally vague, "gradually creates its own filling;" "it is not like that of a pleasure which a man retains

---

[1] "Of what ultimate well-being may be we are unable to say anything but that it must be the complete fulfilment of our capabilities."

from an experience which he has had and would like to have again." The desire for good "acting in us to begin with as a demand which is ignorant of what will satisfy itself, only arrives at a more definite consciousness of its own nature through reflection on its own creations—on habits and institutions and modes of life which, as a demand not reflected upon, it has brought into being."[1] The desire for good cannot be satisfied by merely external advantages; nor by any sum of pleasures; nor by increase of knowledge. It needs the completest activity for human faculty, such as only can be realized in a perfect society of rational, self-conscious persons. Towards this society we are tending. Laws, science, art, religion, are so to speak the incarnations of good. But for the individual, mere compliances with the formal requirements of these social products does not constitute good. For him the good lies, as Kant taught, in the good-will. His good is to seek the good as far as he knows it.

"No good is certain, but the steadfast mind,
The undivided will to seek the good."

Yet for each of us the social arrangements are the true guide to what is good. The popular morality, with its definitions and rules, is a record of past moral judgments, which "becomes a source of new practical direction when applied by a conscience working under a felt necessity of seeking the best, to circumstances

[1] Green, "Prolegomena to Ethics," p. 259.

previously non-existent or not considered, or to some new lesson of experience." (Green, "Proleg.," p. 336-7.)

§ 10. The Æsthetic View.

The ancient Greek view of ethics, which is to be found in Plato and Aristotle, is in marked antithesis to most modern systems. For the Greek thinker, morality was based on no theological or metaphysical presuppositions. His religion gave no basis for his ethics; for him the categorical imperative did not exist. But it was natural to assume that just as in particular parts of the field of conduct—the special arts and crafts—perfection is to be sought, so in the totality of conduct we must aim at the best. All human action is done for some end, and the action is approved according to the degree in which it achieves this end. If human action is to be fundamentally reasonable there must be a supreme end, a *summum bonum*, or a cycle of goods; and this once recognized, it is obviously reasonable to systematize our conduct as a whole, to pay attention to it, so that our entire activity may be best adapted to secure the end. Thus the attitude of the moral man becomes that of an artist. He desires to make his life as good as it can be made. He is indeed at once the artist and the product.

This is not the place to give a detailed account of Greek ethics.[1] Let us rather, without aiming at

[1] Sidgwick, "History of Ethics," chap. ii.

historical accuracy, attempt to give a sketch of what might have been in the mind of Aristotle, or rather what may be in the mind of one of his modern disciples if such there be.

What is the ultimate end of reasonable conduct need not be absolutely determined. If we take some end external to the conduct itself, such as happiness or perfection of our being, our art of life will be analogous to the lower arts, such as cookery or surgery, which seek to achieve some definite external result, and have no further object. But if we take perfection of the conduct itself as our end, if as Aristotle or his editor seems to mean in one passage ("Nich. Eth.," IV. ii.), the end lies in the action itself, our art of life will be like one of the fine arts. We cannot give for a statue or a picture a reason which lies outside the statue or picture itself. The beauty or perfection of the work is its own *raison d'être*.

What, then, will be the standard by which we are to judge the beauty of the conduct?

There is no absolute standard of beauty in art. We perceive beauty; and in this perception thought, implicit rather than explicit, bears the chief part.[1] Hence there will be differences of opinion; our previous knowledge, our power of attention, our capacity for inference, our points of keen interest, our susceptibility to sense-impressions all vary. This want of unanimity, however, does not justify anyone in maintaining that beauty is subjective and unreal, a matter of custom

[1] Sully, "Outlines of Psychology," pp. 366 *seq.*

and fashion and habit. The relativity after all is not, if one may use the expression, an absolute relativity. It can be explained on rational grounds. The child's sense of beauty is not at hopeless variance with the artist's, because the former, as a rule, prefers brighter and purer colours than the latter. The preference of the artist arises from the fact that he recognizes the need of harmony and proportion; he comprehends the work as a whole, while the child neglects all but one part at a time. The well-marked tune which delights the servant-girl palls on the musician; not be-because he has no delight in rhythm, but because this effect is so hackneyed, so facile, and so tiring. In the same way the artist in conduct rejects certain kinds of good conduct which have an attraction for those who think little and feel little. He is ennuyed by cheap effects; by the heedless courage or the heedless generosity which appeals to the admiration of the vulgar. Not that he considers courage and generosity in themselves unworthy of admiration, but that they are, when excessive, incompatible with prudence, true regard for others, modesty, and other qualities of a less striking kind. The ultimate standard, then, of excellence in conduct, as in other acts, will lie in the judgment of the expert. ὁ φρόνιμος, as Aristotle saw, must decide delicate points.[1] A consensus of educated opinion will of course carry great weight; and if anyone complains that this is insufficient, it is well to remember that the area of

[1] "Nic. Eth.," II. 619. Cf. Mill, "Utilitarianism," chap. ii.

controversy is very limited; and further, that whether satisfactory or not, such consensus of experts is all that the average man (or, indeed, any man) has to go on in medicine, law, politics, theology, or science. There is no absolute in knowledge nor in action. "Probability," as Bishop Butler says, "is the guide of life." Be it observed that every thoughtful man is to some extent an expert in matters of conduct, and is entitled to weigh his opinion with that of others. But he will give chief consideration to the maxims drawn by induction from the almost infinite moral observation of the whole human race, checking these by the criticism of poets, and saints, and philosophers. There is, however, no absolute authority in art or in morals as there is in law. The question is always liable to be re-opened, for there is no fixed court of appeal whose decision is necessarily right because it is final.

This ethical method differs from the jural method because it does not pre-suppose the existence of absolute rules. There is no doubt in every doubtful case a way which is, on the whole, the best, if we can only arrive at it; but there is seldom some general formula which is applicable to this case to the exclusion of all other formulas. Our actual solution of the difficulty is almost bound to be to some extent unsatisfactory.

§ 11. Objections to the Æsthetic View.

(1.) To this view the first obvious objection is that the analogy between art and morality is misleading. The artist must produce something; he must have something to show for his labour. But, in reply, it may be said that all arts do not terminate in the production of a visible or tangible object. The executive musician and the actor are acknowledged to be artists; and it must be allowed that a good deed is as much an *object* as a beautiful tune improvised by a musician and incapable of exact repetition, or an admirable performance on the stage.

(2.) The mention of the actor suggests another objection. It will be said that this view makes the appearance the chief thing. Morality becomes on this system a mere performance. The moral artist will aim at the production of external effects, and will be no more bound to really be what he appears to be than is the dramatic artist.

In reply, it must be at once conceded that the danger of make-believe and hypocrisy will exist. The inferior artist is always liable to put forward work which looks right, but will not bear the inspection of experts. But that danger exists on any system of morality, nor would the æsthetic attitude materially increase the temptation. The truly beautiful conduct, the only conduct which the artist will aim at producing, is conduct which is beautiful in motive, intention, and execution. An act externally beautiful, yet not done from a high motive, is not morally admirable in a marked degree. If a merchant gives one of his clerks £5 at Christmas through some mistake which he cannot easily put right without appearing mean, his generosity is obviously only in appearance; if he gives the £5 because he thinks he will get more work out of the clerk, although the act is not disgraceful, it is not a brilliant example of moral beauty; if, however, the employer gives his Christmas-box with the hope that the young man will misuse it— get drunk, and justify his dismissal—the act is morally ugly. In other words, certain internal conditions, such as the motive and intention, are part of the beautiful object which the artist in conduct seeks to produce. And so Aristotle lays down.[1]

(3.) Another objection has already been suggested. It is sometimes difficult to distinguish between the æsthetic aspects of character which are not moral and those that are. There is a certain splendour and fascination about great criminals; the life of a Borgia has been called "beautiful as a tempest."[2] The career of a Napoleon seems more beautiful than that of the industrious citizen who fulfils all his everyday duties with cheerfulness and patience.

The reply to this lies partly in the contrast between the real ethical beauty as recognized by the expert, and the imperfect ethical beauty which appeals to the

---

[1] "Nic. Eth.," II. iv.
[2] See Sidgwick's address to Ethical Society at Cambridge ("Spectator," Aug. 11th, 1888).

insensitive and the thoughtless. There are some excellencies which appeal to all—such as dashing courage, constant activity, brilliant resourcefulness, good-natured though momentary liberality. That these are virtues the expert does not deny; but he recognizes their partial character, and their frequent incompatibility with more important virtues.

If cruel vindictiveness or selfish lust is said to be an artistically beautiful motive, this is probably because we do not put ourselves into close enough relation with the case. We do not adequately realize what must be the interior of a mind in which this emotion is supreme. We do not picture clearly the daily conduct of a person actuated by such an impulse.

Then there is the glamour of successful achievement which is not a reason for moral approval; but which produces a feeling easily confounded with it. Besides, there is the fact that our approved moral ideals sometimes are unduly lacking in the more active and spontaneous elements which once formed part of them, and which the common sense of mankind still admires. Our moral taste, by a natural reaction from the romantic and military and saintly ideals, has become a little bourgeois. The well-behaved classes are just now apt to canonize successful merchants, and to look askance at successful soldiers. It seems as though this one-sidedness, against which the instincts of the crowd have in their crude fashion been a natural protest, were likely to be corrected.

It is clear that on the æsthetic system which

regards moral excellence as akin to beauty, and regards good conduct as an art, the term right undergoes some change in meaning. There is no conduct which here and now can be known as the absolutely and materially right. But we may be able to say with sufficient definiteness that "this conduct is the best open to us, it will avoid more evil and secure more good than any other possible conduct, so far as can be foreseen."

In this way we comply with Professor Sidgwick's dictum: "That there is in any given circumstances some one thing which ought to be done and that this can be known, is a fundamental assumption made not by philosophers only, but by all men who perform any processes of moral reasoning."[1]

This is what we find in the case of other arts; we can never say a particular picture is absolutely right; but we can as a rule decide which picture of several is on the whole the best, considering the conditions under which it is produced. This is best in colour, that in drawing; this in beauty of style, that in earnestness of treatment. So of acts, we cannot say that any act is absolutely right; but this is best in purity of motive, that in prudence of conception; this in cheerfulness of sacrifice, that in equity of purpose.

Thus, too, there remains no categorical imperative. All imperatives are hypothetical. The idea of the

[1] "Methods," bk. i., p. 6 (1st edition). The passage is now omitted; but Dr. Sidgwick apparently does not consider the alteration of material importance.

categorical imperative is due to an illegitimate extension of an essentially relative idea. Reason can order us to do nothing which is not a means to some end.

This theory of ethics is intuitional only in the sense that according to it we perceive the moral beauty of action as we perceive the physical beauty of things: viz., by a process of perception, in which there is an element of thought, but of implicit thought. In all perception there is classification or inference: but it is automatic and unconscious. From these perceptions of ourselves and others we can gather by induction general moral truths. And from these inductively acquired truths we can proceed to verify or correct our perceptions.[1]

[1] See pp. 12-13 above.

CHAPTER VI.

THE PSYCHOLOGY OF ETHICS.

§ 1. Connection between Psychology and Ethics.

The interconnections between Psychology and Ethics are various, and somewhat confusing. The main thing to be kept in mind is that Psychology is purely descriptive, while Ethics is practical and regulative. Psychology indicates the elements, and describes the origin and growth of moral feelings or judgments simply as facts of consciousness, it has nothing to do with their objective validity or invalidity. Ethics, on the other hand, takes from Psychology the terminology which she uses; she accepts the account which Psychology gives of what takes place when we think, or feel, or act. Any statement of an ideal, or rule of conduct, must be necessarily couched in psychological language. Again, the study of the conditions of human activity is necessary to show us what conduct is possible, and hence what conduct is the best. The discovery of what men do desire, and how they do act, cannot indeed answer for us the questions as to what they ought to desire, and how they ought to act, but it is a necessary preliminary to this determination.

This is obvious. But there has been also an illegitimate intrusion of Psychology into the sphere of Ethics, caused by the specific ethical doctrine held by some thinkers as to the grounds of moral distinctions. In the writings of the eighteenth-century moralists, this confusion between the two sciences is very common. The inquiry into the nature and origin of the moral faculty often occupies the largest part of their ethical treatises. This purely psychological inquiry was actually called "the Theory of Morals," as Reid tells us,[1] while he adds, with his usual common sense, that "it has little connection with the knowledge of our duty." "It is," he says, "a very important part of the philosophy of the human mind (*i.e.*, Psychology), and ought to be considered as such, but not as any part of morals." The intuitionalists of the period believed that their doctrine somehow depended on certain psychological views as to the faculty which was held to immediately apprehend the moral quality of actions or the truth of moral judgments. The hedonists attacked their psychology as the most easy way of upsetting their ethical conclusions. Nowadays the whole discussion is felt to be unsatisfactory. The validity of a judgment cannot be *settled* by an inquiry into its origin, although a knowledge of the origin may help us in determining the amount of credence we may provisionally give to it.

[1] Works, ed. Hamilton, p. 642, b.

To assign the elements which can be detected in a complex state of consciousness and to trace the development of the psychosis through lower forms is not the only thing to be done. A living being *is* something more than a mechanical mixture of oxygen, hydrogen, nitrogen, carbon, and so forth; a scientific concept or a moral emotion *is* something more than the elements into which the psychologist analyses it. There is room for another analysis which shall estimate the objective meaning and import of the psychosis as it exists here and now.

§ 2. The Moral Faculty.

Psychologists have analysed mind into intellect, emotion, and will. These are all concerned in morality; not only in the production of moral action, but also in the perception of moral truth. For we must remember that the faculties are abstractions. The intellect does not think, nor the emotions feel. The whole man thinks and feels and acts; and in all moral apprehension there are elements of intellect, emotion, and conation. Of course any judgment or perception must in the main be an intellectual state; that is, the intellectual elements will be the most specialized and important. But the concrete state of mind, the psychosis, is a living whole.

> "Affections, Instincts, Principles, and Powers,
> Impulse and Reason, Freedom and Control,
> So men, unravelling God's harmonious whole,
> Rend in a thousand shreds this life of ours.

> Vain labour! Deep and broad, where none may see,
> Spring the foundations of that shadowy throne,
> Where man's one nature, queen-like, sits alone,
> Centred in a majestic unity."
>
> MATTHEW ARNOLD.

We have already alluded to the intrusion of discussions on the nature of the moral faculty which characterizes eighteenth-century moral philosophy in England. It is interesting to see how this intrusion came to take place.

As long as Ethics was looked upon as the art of conduct, as a rationalizing of life, there was no need to suppose any special capacity for apprehending moral facts, because moral facts were not in kind different from other facts. When the jural view of Ethics began to obtain, owing to the influence of Roman law, and the influence of the Jewish scriptures, which formed a part of the Christian text-book of morality, an attempt was made to find out what laws were binding on all men *quâ* men. Sir H. Maine has shown how the prætorian judges, stimulated by the Stoic philosophy, gave origin to the ideal of a *jus naturale*, which, as it were, lay behind the particular and specific laws of individual states. In the same way, the Christian theologians were influenced in their turn by the new ideal; they assumed the existence of a code of natural morality, binding on all men and implicitly contained in the customs and positive laws of all races of men. They distinguished this from the Jewish code, and from the ecclesiastical code binding on Christians, as well as from the code of state law. What was felt to be obligatory by all was part of the original moral deposit. The conscience was the test or criterion of the natural code. What the conscience forbade was forbidden by God universally for all men. Thus the nature of conscience or moral faculty became a supremely interesting point. It was clearly something very special—something different from the rest of human nature, since its deliverances were practically revelations of the will of God. It was not dependent on the accidents of education; but was clearly innate, given to every man by God as a light to conduct.

This innateness was denied by Locke; who, however, undoubtedly misunderstood the doctrine he attacked. Broadly speaking, the Schoolmen and the Platonists, *e.g.* More and Cudworth, taught not that there existed ready-made moral ideas in the minds of children and savages; but that there existed at birth a moral faculty which was capable of development. That they attached too little importance to the need of education and experience may be true, but they did not as a rule deny it.

§ 3. Moral Sense.

The term "sense of right and wrong" was used by Shaftesbury to indicate the "reflecting faculty" which in rational beings takes notice of their various impulses and approves or disapproves them according as they are good or bad. Shaftesbury was no psychologist;

and he does not make clear whether this "sense" was mainly of the nature of thought or of the nature of emotion; whether it was like Locke's internal sense, *i.e.*, introspective consciousness, or whether it was simply a form of emotion, the cause of which lay not in external objects but in the affections (or impulses) themselves. Probably he thought of it as at once perceptive and emotional.

The moral sense doctrine was developed by Hutcheson and other writers. There was in the middle of the eighteenth century a growing tendency to lay stress on emotion. In England it is found in the writings of the novelists, Richardson, Sterne, and Mackenzie, as well as in the formal treatises of the moral-sense school. On the continent it is especially associated with the name of Rousseau. Connected with it was the general tendency of psychologists, lasting till the middle of the present century, to analyse all intellectual acts into subjective associations of feelings.

Judgment itself was looked on as a mere association of impressions, immediate or remembered. Hence the most prominent and tangible factor in the complex state we call moral approbation became the emotion which accompanies the perception; just as the perception of the beautiful was resolved into feeling.

Neither Hutcheson nor Hume denies that there is an element of judgment or perception in the apprehension of moral quality. But they both assert that the distinctive and peculiar feature of this apprehension was the presence of a special kind of emotion, akin to that which accompanies the apprehension of the beautiful. By virtue Hume means "whatever mental action or quality gives to the spectator the pleasing sentiment of approbation." "Crime or immorality is no particular fact or relation which can be the object of the understanding; but arises entirely from the sentiment of disapprobation which, by the structure of human nature, we unavoidably feel on the apprehension of barbarity or treachery."[1]

The specific character of moral quality was forgotten; indeed, it was resolved into utility; just as æsthetic quality was resolved into utility by other members of the same school. But the unguarded language used led to the belief which is expressed by Reid that "Mr. Hume will have the moral sense to be only a power of feeling without judging;" which he rightly objects to as an abuse of the word "sense."

Modern writers commonly refrain from the use of this ambiguous term. Whether moral apprehension be of the nature of external perception, as Reid maintained, or like the recognition of beauty as Shaftesbury maintained, the word "sense" is inapplicable.

§ 4. Moral Reason.

What then is the part played by the intellect in the apprehension of moral quality?

The perception of the external acts which constitute conduct is, of course, primarily intellectual; and so is

[1] Hume, "Essays," pp. 480-483 (Ward and Lock).

the self-conscious recognition of motives, volitions, feelings, which we call internal perception. The recognition of the relations between the outer facts, between the inner facts, and between the two groups, is intellectual: *e.g.* the recognition that a given act is a means to a given end. Any moral apprehension which can be thrown into the form of a judgment is necessarily an intellectual act; nor, as we have just seen, was this really denied by Hume. To say that such moral quality is apprehended by reason [1] is only to affirm that it is objective, that it does not exist for me alone, but for all minds.

We must distinguish between the discursive and the intuitive employment of reason in matters of morality. When we infer that a given ethical proposition is true because of its connection with some other ethical proposition; when we recognize a given act as good or right because it leads to some end, or an end as good because it leads to some more ultimate end, we are exercising reason discursively.

But we naturally assume that our chain of inferences is not self-supporting; that it is somewhere fastened to a point of support, some staple in the wall. There cannot, we feel, be endless retrogression. Inference must terminate in intuition, in the recognition of some ultimate major premise. If our knowledge as a whole is justifiable at the bar of reason this premise must be justifiable. In other words, Reason

[1] By Reason we mean the completest and most thorough employment of our intelligence.

can guarantee the ultimate premise; there is such a faculty as intuitive reason. The existence of discursive reason implies it.

For examples of such ultimate ethical premises we may refer to chap. v., §§ 4 and 5. And even if we allege that the knowledge is self-supporting, that the system rests on nothing external but maintains itself by virtue of its own inner relations (like the solar system or the vortex-ring), the acceptance of this point of view itself is due to something more than ordinary reasoning; it is the selection of a starting-point as in itself less needing justification than the judgments dependent on it.

This rational starting point in Ethics may be (1) the immediate recognition of moral quality in acts or motives; or (2) the immediate recognition of moral truth in judgments. The former is merely moral perception; it is not simple and ultimate, but contains implicit judgment like all other kinds of perception. All we mean by the moral quality perceived, is the relation that the given act bears to our ideals of conduct. This relation (or rather set of relations) is analogous to those which subsist in the case of an object of external perception viewed in its æsthetic aspect. Whatever be the origin of our moral perceptions there is no doubt we have them now; any more than there is doubt that we immediately perceive objects as beautiful or ugly.

The second kind of intuitive apprehension is the recognition of the truth of ultimate general propositions which are incapable of being supported by further inference: which must, at any rate for the given discussion, be taken as final. This has been sufficiently illustrated in the chapter on Intuition.

Reason (*i.e.* the intellectual powers in their completest form) has more to do with conduct than simply to give us ethical principles and ethical conclusions. It has a practical as well as theoretical function, for it serves as a guide or regulator of action. Before a course of action is determined on, we require to know that it is possible. A civilized man is capable of consistent action for an end, or in obedience to a rule. Although this purposive consistency of action which constitutes conduct does not constitute the whole of virtue (since, to give no other reason, it may be for a bad end), it forms a very large part of virtue. This systematization is due to Reason, which suppresses impulses that lead astray or are in direct conflict with the means necessary to secure the ends aimed at.

Besides all this, Reason may be called a spring of action. Reid, Stewart, and other philosophers have regarded the practical function of Reason as merely directive and regulative. It suppresses what is irrational and therefore wrong, but it cannot, they say, originate action. In the same way some modern thinkers allege that Reason cannot give an end, it can only give us the means to an end which is demanded by active impulse.[1] But most people will agree that a man may act from principle as well

[1] Gizycki and Coit, pp. 85 *seq.*

as feeling. A vivid perception that a certain course of conduct is in conflict with a recognized law leads a man to give it up; although his mere feelings may be wholly on the side of the prohibited line of action. Kant indeed actually asserted that no other kind of right-doing is really virtuous; it is only when we do right because it is right, and not because we want to do it or take pleasure in it, that, strictly speaking, we are doing right at all. It is certain that in a properly constituted mind the perception that an action is right is an irresistible motive for doing it; but whether the motive lies in the mere intellectual state itself or is rather to be ascribed to the specific emotion accompanying such a state, is not so easily decided. With all use of reason is bound up emotion. The distinction between intellect and emotion is indeed like all other analysis, a logical device. In nature continuity is always present. We must not forget that in moral, as well as in other matters, man judges and acts as man and not like a logic machine.

Intellect is thus a spring of action. We act in a certain way because we recognize that way as right. It matters not whether we say that the intellectual act itself is the motive, or that the intellectual act is accompanied by a specific desire, the desire to act rationally, and that this is the actual motive power. For ethical purposes the two statements are equivalent.

Moral reason, then, which simply means reason as concerned with morals, has a fourfold office:

(i) It recognizes moral facts and moral principles.
(ii) It draws conclusions.
(iii) It systematizes conduct.
(iv) It is an impulse to action.

§ 5. Moral Emotions.

Moral emotion is one of the highest and most complex forms of feeling, belonging to the special class of feelings known as sentiments, *i.e.*, " non-personal emotions which gather about certain objects and ideas common to all."[1]

Strictly speaking, there are several allied emotions, having objects which are more or less connected, and forming a tolerably well-marked group.

(1.) The moral sentiment proper—the desire to do right as such, the feeling of necessity and obligation which arises when we recognize a certain course as right. This is the most specifically ethical emotion. " Moral approval or disapproval differs from æsthetic in that it always fastens on a human action, whether another's or our own, and on that particular aspect or relation of the action which we call its rightness or wrongness. It is thus pre-eminently a *practical, i.e.* action-controlling, feeling."[2] It is peculiarly associated with the jural view of Ethics; and is clearly connected with the religious emotions. In fact, if morality had not been developed under theological conditions as a

---

[1] Sully, "Outlines," p. 520 (1st edition). See p. 360 in new edition.

[2] *Ibid.*, p. 368 (new edition).

divine system of natural law, this specific emotion could hardly have come into existence. Now that it has come into existence, it does not seem impossible to transfer it to a more æsthetic or perfectionist view of conduct.

When we recognize a course of conduct as right, we immediately feel it binding on us and on others. This feeling is so closely associated with the recognition of conduct as right, that the intellectual apprehension itself appears to be a motive to action. (See this chapter, § 4.)

(2.) The sentiments of approbation for particular kinds of moral conduct and disapprobation of the opposite. As Professor Sully says, "A difference in the nature . . . . of the action affects our feeling towards it. Thus, different kinds of bad or good conduct excite different shades of moral feeling."[1] These particularized kinds of moral feeling are called by Dr. Sidgwick the "quasi-moral sentiments," because, although normally associated with the moral sentiment proper, the desire to do right as such, they are sometimes in conflict with it. The love for veracity in the priest or the teacher may have to be mortified, in a case where some amount of untruthfulness seems incumbent on us. The modesty of a pure-minded woman has sometimes to be suppressed at what she knows to be call of duty.

The quasi-moral sentiments are clearly connected with the æsthetic sentiments—the emotional con-

[1] Sully, "Outlines," p. 557 (1st edit.); cf. also his "Human Mind," vol. ii., pp. 168 *seq*.

L

comitants of our recognition of an act as *pulchrum*. We recognize many other things as beautiful besides virtue; and conduct is often æsthetically satisfying which is ethically wrong.

(3.) The voice of conscience, as it is often called; the remorse, which we feel when the conduct disapproved is our own: and with this may be grouped the feeling of moral self-approbation, which was dwelt on with such emphasis by the eighteenth-century moralists, and by such writers as Addison and Fielding.

We have come to see that the latter sentiment is dangerous to modesty, and liable to make us rest contented with low ideals, so that it no longer occupies the prominent place that it formerly took. But, perhaps, most people are still inclined to attribute too much importance to the feeling of remorse. It should be remembered that all self-blame is not moral. We often regret with peculiar poignancy the perpetration of small slips in grammar and manners; while falls into our besetting sin are often taken somewhat as a matter of course. Again, there is such a thing as morbid exaggeration of conscientiousness, where the sentiment of self-remorse suffers from a sort of hyperæsthesia. Some earnest souls are always finding fault with themselves out of measure, about the smallest matters. Their most venial slips pain them so much that they become despondent, and even peevish and ill-tempered. Such distorted and excessive regret for our past conduct is a serious bar to further improvement.

§ 6. Conscience.

As used by ordinary folk, conscience often means little more than a particular judgment on one's conduct, together with that form of moral emotion last described, viz. remorse for one's own recognized wrongdoing. In this sense it is personal, and implies no objective validity. Used in a wider sense it covers moral cognition with the accompanying approbation and disapprobation, as when we say in advance, "I cannot do that, it is against my conscience." It is simply the moral faculty, and this is the sense in which it is most frequently used by intuitive moralists, usually with an implication that the moral judgment and emotion refer to our own acts.

Such moralists have usually maintained that it is intuitive, underived, and universal. That our moral cognitions are not always immediate has already been shown (chap. i., § 3). That like the outcome of other innate capacities of thought and feeling, our moral judgments and emotions are partly due to the reaction of society on the individual, is easily seen. This fact in itself would lead us to expect that moral judgments and feelings will differ in different ages and among different races of men; and observation shows that this is the case. But we may fairly assert that conscience is universal, in the sense that no race has been discovered which is entirely without judgments of conduct as right and wrong, and accompanying emotions. That the matter of the judgments and the nature of the emotions vary does not disprove this.[1]

The psychological question as to the origin of our moral emotions which has been referred to above, may be expressed in the following way:—Do I feel bound not to steal, do I loathe the idea of stealing, because my ancestors and myself have found that stealing leads to unpleasant consequences to us? Or in other words, is our conscience due to "the experience of social discipline?"

The general drift of modern opinion answers this question in the affirmative. Our egoistic hatred of pain leads us to shrink from what brings on us physical suffering, whether due to the unconscious action of external things, or the conscious action of parents, governors, or magistrates. It leads us to shrink from risking disapproval of others, whether expressed in a slight and negative way, by rigorous social ostracism, or by outspoken condemnation. Thus conscience comes to be the reflection within of the external government and the opinion of society. We come to shrink quite automatically from what is associated with such physical or mental pain. And these factors have been always in action since society began to exist. Private revenge and public authority have helped to cut off undesirable members of society, and the forces of selection and heredity have helped to intensify and widen that "imitation of the government without us" which we call conscience. The

[1] Compare the relativity of the æsthetic faculty.

authority of society is exercised by parents and teachers as well as by the civil magistrate. The suppression of impulse in accordance with the command of others is a necessary step in the formation of conscience. The life of the well-ordered family and school with its opportunities of rivalry and of affection plays an important part in the development.[1]

Thus mingled with these purely egoistic elements due to the discipline of society, are others of a more altruistic character. The desire for the company and the esteem of others is only in part egoistic; it is an important example of the ego-altruistic group of feelings. And the effects of sympathy, of direct and spontaneous desire for the wellbeing of others, are of considerable importance in the later development of conscience, though probably they have small influence in the earlier stages of civilization. Other moral co-cperatives, as Stewart calls them, are feelings of reverence, and the æsthetic feelings.

In the same way the sentiment of beauty is perhaps developed from purely animal feelings, the delight in play due to surplus of animal energy. But this does not make us question the validity and objectivity of our æsthetic judgments, nor need the comparatively lowly origin of our moral sentiment throw doubt on the reality of morality.

[1] On the growth of the moral faculty see Sully, " Outlines," pp. 369-371 ; " Human Mind," vol. ii., pp. 161-166.

§ 7. Pleasure and Desire.

As sympathy is the most important of the moral co-operatives, and as most systems of ethics, especially the traditional Christian view, lay stress on the duty of unselfish regard for others, an important psychological question may be here noticed.

It has been almost universally assumed by Hedonists, and frequently by other writers, that all our actions are necessarily directed towards the attainment of pleasure and the avoidance of pain. If this be so we can never be really unselfish, for all our acts are self-regarding, determined, as Bentham says, by our two sovereign masters, pleasure and pain. Cynical writers have insisted that even justice and benevolence can be resolved into a far-sighted regard for our interest. The virtuous man is benevolent because doing good to others is a source of satisfaction to himself. Such a view we feel to be extravagantly paradoxical, although we may be ready to grant with Aristotle that not only does the truly virtuous man take pleasure in good actions, but that he would not be really virtuous unless he did so.

The assertion that our own pleasure (or avoidance of pain) is the object of all our volition is open to grave doubt. Butler long ago pointed out in opposition to the "licentious reasoners" of the school of Mandeville, that we must make a distinction between self-love, the desire of happiness for ourselves, and the particular desires directed towards particular objects.[1] Our impulses are naturally directed towards things. Pleasure may be aimed at, but this is a new feature in conduct which may be superinduced in the simpler desires, which indeed it really assumes and implies. I desire my own pleasure, but what *is* my pleasure except the gratification of my desires? The experience of pleasure is not more often the antecedent of desire, than the experience of desire is antecedent to the existence of pleasure. There are some pleasures which can only be attained by artificially stimulating the growth of a desire, as in the case of gambling, fox-hunting, and stamp-collecting.[2] Again, desires often bear no proportion to the pleasures which arise from their gratification; as Dr. Ward puts it, they become "more imperious, though less productive of pleasure as time goes on." And some desires we seem to have before we can be supposed to remember the pleasures which their gratification produces; for the child desires food long before we can suppose it to have any mental representation of the "ideal pleasure" of satisfied hunger.

Those who hold the view that all desire is ultimately directed towards pleasure indeed admit: (1) that through association we may come to desire objects for themselves alone, at least so far as introspection can discover, and (2) that in the special case of "fixed ideas" we may aim at what is not conceived

---

[1] "Sermons on Human Nature," I.
[2] Hence the Hedonistic Paradox, that the best way to secure happiness is not to aim at it directly.

as pleasure giving. These two concessions in point of fact give up the very point at issue. If in these two cases it is possible to desire something else than pleasure, clearly the allegation that all conduct is directed towards self-gratification falls to the ground. Dr. Bain now indeed allows the existence of a rhythm in consciousness between extra-regarding and self-regarding impulses. But it is a somewhat bizarre view of human nature which suggests that all altruistic conduct and a great deal which is neither altruistic nor egoistic is irrational, and is due to a morbid volitional condition akin to that which leads a weak man to throw himself over a cliff, or a hypnotic patient to try to swim for his life when he is sprawling on my turkey carpet. There is no need for such a violent hypothesis. The existence of altruistic feelings is as obvious, and as easily explained on evolutionary principles, as the existence of egoistic feelings.[1]

Of course in a sense all my desires are selfish because they are mine, because they aim at securing objects of the need of which I am conscious and not you. But in this sense all my thoughts are selfish because they are mine. It seems more satisfactory to restrict the term to desires which directly aim at what will give us pleasure *because* it will give us pleasure, to acts in which " the ego is not only the source of the volition but also its object." The attempt to represent the martyr as enduring the

[1] Spencer, "Principles of Ethics," vol. i., pp. 203 *seq.*

§ 8. Motive and Intention.

agonies of martyrdom for the sake of the intense spiritual pleasure which accompanies them, is a very poor psychological joke.

There is considerable uncertainty in the use of these two words. Austin, whose analysis is of course made from the point of view of the lawyer, defines motive as " a wish causing or preceding a volition," in other words, as equivalent to definite desire. And by intention he means the expected effect of an action, whether wished or merely expected. Thus intention includes those consequences which we would rather did not happen, as well as those which we wish to produce. If nausea is an inevitable consequence of my taking a dose of medicine, and I know it, I intend the nausea, though I do not wish it. This refinement in the meaning is not quite in keeping with ordinary usage. When we speak of intention we ordinarily mean the intended and desired effects of an action.

Motive is thus reserved for the mainly emotional condition, " the conscious impulse to action, whether desire or aversion," as Professor Sidgwick defines it, while intention is reserved for the objective effects aimed at.

Motive is, however, often used for the end aimed at, the idea of the object desired, instead of the impulse itself. It is so employed, for instance, by Mr.

Muirhead, who defines motive as "the idea of the object which, through congruity with the character of the self, moves the will."[1] It seems unsatisfactory to give up a meaning which, on the whole, was a convenient one, and which was accepted by lawyers as well as moralists. But the transition from one meaning to the other is not uncommon in ordinary usage, and can be easily accounted for.

In the words of Professor Sully, "A motive is a desire viewed in its relation to a particular represented action, to the carrying out of which it urges or prompts. The desire in this case ceases to be a vague, fluctuating state of longing, and becomes fixed and defined as an impulse to realize a definite concrete experience, viz., the known and anticipated result of a particular action; or, since the object of desire is now fore-grasped as the certain result of a particular active exertion, it assumes the form of the *end* of this action."[2]

It should be noticed that we seldom, if ever, act from a single motive. Dr. Sidgwick's emancipated Jew, who eats bacon from a "desire to vindicate true religious liberty combined with a liking for pork," is a type of most good men. It is not so much the martyr as the madman whose motive is absolutely single. Even when we overrule an impulse it usually helps to colour the imperious and predominant feeling which led to its suppression. These considerations are important in

---

[1] "Elements of Ethics," p. 58.
[2] "Human Mind," vol. ii., p. 208.

connection with Dr. Martineau's special form of intuitionism already alluded to.[1]

§ 9. Freedom of the Will.

The chief question which ethics raises with regard to the will is not so much a psychological as a metaphysical one. Psychology cannot settle the freedom of the will, because like all other sciences psychology must assume the validity of the categories of thought. It must take notice of the "consciousness of freedom" which we undoubtedly have, and it may explain how this consciousness arises, but it cannot settle the validity of the apparent intuition, although, as Dr. Sully rightly says, such a genetic explanation "would manifestly cut away the psychological ground of the common form of the doctrine of liberty."[2] The question must be left over to the domain of metaphysic, which deals with the final concepts of different departments of knowledge, and examines the assumptions made not only in ordinary thought but in the systematic thinking of the sciences.

What is meant by calling the will free?

(1) That we are free to act as we please, that we can will to act as we see fit to act, that we can will to act as we see it is reasonable to act. This asserts the dependence of volition on thought, but not that

[1] See above, chap. v., § 3.
[2] "Human Mind," vol. ii., p. 365.

volition is caused by thought. When the volition is in agreement with our judgment the volition is free. (2) There is a reference to an I-myself. This, however, is the empirical self, the group of psychological actualities and possibilities which we have come to know as we have come to know other objects of experience. Whether we imply a further and more intimate reference to the pure self, the metaphysical assumption which we seem driven to make as a necessary basis for all psychological explanation, is another matter.

Without attempting a full examination of the question[1] we may note the following points. (1) "The assumption of free-will is in a certain sense inevitable to anyone exercising rational choice."[2] This is admitted by the Determinists but explained away. It merely means that I can act as I please; the action is my action, determined by my nature as a whole and not by any external force or by any one part of my nature to the exclusion of the rest. "The sense of freedom is the realization of the function of consciousness in its most complex and impressive manifestation."[3]

(2) The purely phenomenalist psychology of Mill and his school has completely broken down. We are obliged to allow that there is something in mind besides ideas and motives, viz. the attending mind

[1] See Appendix A, p. 199, for a full list of authorities.
[2] Sidgwick in "Mind," Oct., 1889.
[3] Sully, "Human Mind," vol. ii., p. 293.

itself, the *intellectus ipse.* This admission destroys the force of a great deal of the Associationist polemic.

(3) The mere fact that we can draw no clear line between automatic and voluntary activity proves nothing. This is only another example of the continuity of experience. The inner world is no more made like a set of disconnected pigeon-holes than is the outer. Intelligence passes into instinct, consciousness into unconsciousness, volition into automatism, just as biological species shade off into each other.

(4) On the other hand, one of the most important metaphysical arguments of the Libertarians seems to need reconsideration. Kant urges that our knowledge of our moral responsibility involves the assumption of free-will. I ought, therefore I can. But it is open to question whether any such thing as absolute moral responsibility is conceivable, except on a definitely theistic hypothesis. Unless this theistic basis is supplied the transcendental employment of the essentially relative conception of responsibility seems unwarranted. The categorical imperative turns out to be unthinkable.[1]

Dr. Sidgwick argues that we can construct a theory of ethics without the idea of free-will.[2] The Determinist can give to the terms responsibility, desert, and

---

[1] See above, chap. iii., §§ 5, 9.
[2] "Methods," bk. i., chap. v., § 2. Professor Sidgwick makes an exception with regard to one point. But even this exception has no practical bearing.

so on, perfectly clear and definite meanings. He "allows that in a sense 'ought' implies 'can'; that a man is only morally bound to do what is 'in his power,' and that only acts from which a man 'could have abstained' are proper subjects of punishment or moral condemnation. But he explains 'can' and 'in his power' to imply only the absence of no obstacle that may not be overcome by sufficient motive. It is precisely in such cases, he maintains, that punishment and the expression of moral displeasure are required to supply the desiderated motive force." Virtuous conduct is obligatory when the only obstacle to prevent our following it is the comparative weakness of our moral nature and the comparative strength of our sensuous impulses. As long as a rational man is free from external compulsion he is bound by the laws of morality, and the object of moral discipline is to reinforce the good motives.

It is clear, that whether we believe in freedom or not, we can construct an ethical theory which shall describe the ideally best conduct, the conduct which the wise man will follow because he is wise. But can we further say that it is morally binding on us, that we *ought* to follow it?

We have seen that ought and obligation have a threefold reference. (1) to human law, (2) to divine law, (3) to the ideal law, moral truths under the aspect of rules (chap. iii., § 5). Clearly society may compel me to adopt the ideal conduct it prescribes. Clearly God can compel me to adopt it. Thus the first two senses are quite compatible with Determinism. In the third sense the concept of obligation is extended to cover the relations between the impersonal moral law and the individual who apprehends it. Any moral ideal regarded as desirable for me may be regarded as moral law binding on me. Thus the necessary obligation of a moral truth is not dependent on any metaphysical theory as to the will. The same ideal conduct may be considered *sub specie boni* and *sub specie juris*, according to the way in which we look at it.

§ 10. Habit.

Every movement tends to reproduce itself. The very fact that it has occurred once tends to make it occur again. There remains a pre-disposition to recur, which becomes strengthened by repetition and attention. Gradually consciousness, which is perhaps at first concentrated in order to acquire the habit, diminishes. The act is performed with the smallest amount of consciousness and on the slightest stimulus. Complicated groups and series of movements become welded into a whole; and whether simple or complex they recur with such ease and regularity on the presentation of the appropriate stimulus and with such a minimum of consciousness that such acts are called secondarily automatic.

In order that any really complex and difficult series of actions should be performed easily it is necessary that they should pass from the condition of fully conscious acts into that of habit. This is true of internal activities as well as external. The control over impulses only becomes easy and regular by becoming habitual. Certain feelings are given the preponderance, and take on a new form, that of ruling dispositions.

The importance of habit in conduct was first seen by Aristotle. He regarded virtues as fixed dispositions, or habits of feeling and acting, only to be acquired in the same way as other habits. Modern moralists have overlooked this, and have too much looked on virtue as a matter of mere momentary will. This is partly due to the more subjective attitude of modern philosophers. With Shaftesbury, with Kant, and with the classical Christian moralists of the eighteenth century, the essence of virtue lies in the endeavour to do right. The matter is sacrificed to the form. But real excellence of conduct, as Aristotle saw, is only possible on the same terms as excellence in any specific art. This of course has been seen clearly by teachers and confessors, although somewhat obscured by theoretical moralists and preachers. The latter have felt so strongly the need of individual effort, and they have seen so clearly that the presence of the formal element is necessary, that they have somewhat kept out of sight the need for repetition and practice if our conduct is to attain any really high degree of excellence.

Virtue thus tends to become less conscious. The earliest efforts of the child to control its temper, to be forgiving or just, are painfully full of consciousness, just as they are clumsy and imperfect. Practice makes perfect in morals as well as in other things; and the good man finds no great difficulty in doing what is impossible to the child.

Common sense does not support the view of Kant, that conduct is only virtuous when it is difficult and painful. The forgiveness which is free and instantaneous marks a higher development of virtue than that which is grudging and delayed; although the latter may be more interesting to the teacher or moralist as evincing the beginning of a new moral effort. It is the old story over again. The rejoicing over the returning prodigal is greater than that over the ninety-nine just men who need no repentance. But this does not show that the moral condition of the prodigal is higher than that of the ninety-nine.

§ 11. Is Wrong-doing involuntary?

We have already discussed the conditions of complete responsibility (chap. iii., § 9). Broadly speaking we are only responsible when the act is completely voluntary.

This raises the question, Is vice ever really voluntary? Socrates and Plato answered the question in the negative. We always, says Plato in effect, aim at that which in the moment of action seems the best for us. If we choose a wrong course of action, and abandon the higher satisfaction for the lower, and so become cowardly, or lustful, or unjust, it is because at the moment we choose ignorantly. Our education, and the government under which we live, and our inherited physical and psychical constitution, are the causes of our error. Vice is due to illusion, to the temporary obscuration of the real qualities of things and the real meaning of acts.

This view of the nature of vice has been emphasized by modern thinkers, especially those who have approached the subject from a biological or medical point of view. The tendency is to look at crime as due to physical conditions inherited or acquired, for which society may be in some sense responsible, but hardly the criminal himself.

On the other hand, common sense revolts against the paradox that no man is voluntarily bad. The modern and more subjective spirit, due chiefly to Christianity, recognizes to the full the truth of the poet's

"Video meliora proboque deteriora sequor."

We believe we can resist temptation if we will; and we hesitate to ask if the will is always possible. We know that our weakness of character is largely due to our own acts; and we cannot say for certain that any given individual, not insane or idiotic, was at first so morally incapable as to be absolutely unable to control his vicious inclinations if acted upon by adequate stimuli.[1]

---

[1] We know a man's character may change on being presented

It does not seem possible to regard vice (or virtue) as in the highest sense voluntary—voluntary as the plain man understands the word—unless we start from the doctrine of free-will. The Determinist regards our actions as caused by our desires and feelings; and these in turn are the products of two factors, the one being our environment, including government, society, etc., and the other our innate psychical disposition and tendencies, or, which comes to the same thing, inherited organic structures. If this be so, our acts are the results of causes over which the pure subject, the ultimate Ego, has no control. The empirical self, the character which is built up by the interaction of the two factors, is as much a phenomenon to it as any external object. It sees the wish to improve arise, and sees it carry its point or fail; but the origination of the wish and its success or failure, are not due to the consciousness which watches it.

In a sense we may hold that vice is not entirely voluntary, without minimizing the distinction between good and evil. "They know not what they do," is true of other offenders besides those who crucified the Son of Man. The evil comes in choosing the lower good where the higher is attainable; in the imperfect sympathies and feeble imagination which lead us to prefer the anti-social and the selfish ideals to the altruistic.

with fresh stimuli; and we commonly assume that the man may encounter these stimuli if he wills to do so.

CHAPTER VII.

THE CLASSIFICATION OF MORAL EXCELLENCES.

§ 1. The Consistency of Moral Excellences.

WE have seen that good conduct may be looked at as a system of moral excellences, or as a system of compliance with moral law. But we are naturally anxious to see whether these two respectively (1) cover the whole of good conduct, and (2) can be reduced to one common principle. This involves the problem of the classification of virtues or duties.

The need for the assumption that moral laws cover the whole ground of conduct, and that they are never in real conflict—in other words, the need for continuity and consistency in moral law—is chiefly felt by those who adopt the purely jural view. If we take the other view, and regard virtuous conduct as a sum of excellences, we do not necessarily demand that all of these excellences should be exhibited in their most complete form by the same person. A man, especially if he be a soldier, may be somewhat less temperate than perfection demands, so that he be thoroughly courageous and generous; just as we may excuse deficient technique in a picture, if the drawing and colour and sentiment be beyond praise. We recognize that these different excellences in morality are, like those of art, to some extent mutually exclusive. The different excellences have come to be recognized independently of conscious classification as good, and we are not startled when we realize that they not only overlap, but clash. Prudence, as ordinarily conceived, involves some defect of courage; regard for consequences to oneself is as much of the essence of prudence, as disregard for them is of the essence of courage. The paradox that the prudent man who avoids giving way to anger is really brave, is as untrue as the paradox that after all courage is only cowardice as to the opinion of others.

But this admission can hardly be made if we look at morality as a system of laws all equally binding on us. The jural moralist, like the lawyer, is obliged to assume that his laws are consistent, as well as that they cover the whole ground, that in fulfilling one you cannot be breaking another.

§ 2. Classifications adopted by early Moralists.

Some virtues are evidently subaltern, and can be conveniently placed under others. Thus modesty comes under temperance, while honesty comes under justice, and pity under benevolence. But some of these more specific virtues have a claim to come under two or three of the more generic. Thus patience comes under both temperance and courage, caution under temperance and wisdom, candour under veracity and justice.

Socrates taught that virtue is knowledge—more particularly knowledge of ends, the things really worth seeking. Hence the virtues are essentially one, because they are only applications of wisdom, the supreme excellence, to the varying exigencies of life. Plato's view is more subtle and less simple. He enumerates σοφία, wisdom, ἀνδρεία, courage, σωφροσύνη, temperance, and δικαιοσύνη, justice or uprightness, including law-observance generally. Plato's basis of classification is psychological: σοφία is the special excellence of νοῦς or intellect; ἀνδρεία is the special excellence of θῦμος, or the active impulses; σωφροσύνη that of ἐπιθυμία, the appetitive or concupiscent elements in the soul. These, the "four cardinal virtues" of the Christian moralists,[1] are mentioned in the Alexandrian "Wisdom of Solomon," viii. 7, and their essential unity is recognized.

They are so called, not only as the most important, but because they are generic virtues under which the others may be subserved.

Aristotle's list scarcely rises to the dignity of a classification. It does not discriminate between the higher and the subaltern virtues. It is based on that of Plato, but he adds many minor excellences, and

---

[1] The expression is said to occur first in the writings of St. Ambrose.

considerably limits the generic character of the four supreme virtues recognized by Plato, e.g. ἀνδρεία is confined to war, and σωφροσύνη is applied only to the bodily appetites.

His enumeration is as follows: wisdom, justice, courage, temperance, liberality, magnificence (μεγαλοπρεπεία), highmindedness (μεγαλοψυχία), ambition, gentleness, friendliness, truthfulness, wittiness, and shame. This is a haphazard and somewhat superficial catalogue of excellences, but it has the merit of candour and freshness, and psychological insight. There is a frank recognition of minor characteristics, the absence of which goes far to ruin a hero or a saint. The contempt for small things and the indifference to small economies require a large fortune to back them. We cannot all be Portias. Aristotle holds with Wordsworth that

> "High Heaven rejects the lore
> Of nicely calculated less or more."

But there is a touch of Sir Gorgius Midas, a slight suggestion of vulgarity, in the magnificent man, as conceived by the rich philosopher. In the same way his highminded man although realized at his best in Dante, is not without some resemblance to the heroes of Ouida. The demand that the perfectly virtuous man shall have εὐτραπελία is perhaps least in keeping with the spirit of Hebraism which survives in our religion, and the moral earnestness which is the special pride of the age. But after all has it not been said, that no man has ever become a great saint without a sense of humour?

The common bond by which Aristotle professes to link the virtues is the doctrine of the μεσότης. But it breaks down hopelessly and confessedly in the case of several of the virtues.

To the virtues recognized by the heathen world, Christians added humility, which was hardly a virtue to the Greeks and Romans; purity, as opposed to mere temperance; and the three "theological virtues," faith, hope, and love, of which the only one purely ethical is the last. This had not been quite adequately recognized by the philosophers, whose morality was a little self-centred. At the same time it is important to point out that among the late Stoics there had already been a great development in the same direction. Pity and purity had begun to take their place by the side of the robuster virtues.

The ordinary Christian moralists (for instance, Dante, as the representative of mediæval thought, and Paley, as representative of modern thought) recognize a division of excellences of conduct or duties (for the prevailing view is the jural one) into three groups: towards God, our neighbour, and ourself. But of course all duties are, on the Christian theory, in a sense owed to God, indirectly if not directly; and it is the distinctly theological, as opposed to the moral, duties which are specially owed to Him. Moral duties then fall into two divisions, extra-regarding and self-regarding. To the former belong justice, truth, benevolence; to the latter, temperance, purity, courage, and prudence, each with its subsidiary excellences. Even this distinction cannot be rigidly maintained, for intemperance, impurity, and suicide are offences against others and against society, as well as against ourselves; while many acts of injustice and untruthfulness (*e.g.* fraudulent railway travelling in a superior class) are chiefly reprehensible because of their effect on the offender himself.

§ 3. Duties to Self and to our Neighbour.

It is often said that all morality is social.[1] To determine " how the individual agent is related to the society in which he lives " is regarded as the complete answer to the question, " What do we mean by good and bad, right and wrong, in reference to conduct ? " Even our duties to self are regarded as indirectly owed to society. " If they all of them alike seem to be so little social in character it is because as the individual becomes the centre of interest they concern him in relations which extend beyond the most familiar form of society, the nation, and bind him simply as a man with other men." The evil effects of secret bad conduct are ultimately social. They diminish the social efficiency of the evil-doer. This may indeed be admitted. We may allow that the individual can never shake himself free from his dependence on

---

[1] See Alexander, "Moral Order and Progress," pp. 81 *seq.*, 119 *seq.*

society. The mere individual is an ethical myth. Our dependence on society is so absolute that we can never even imagine a man who owes nothing to it. Language, to mention nothing else, constitutes such a bond between each of us and society that we see such things, and think such thoughts, and feel such feelings, as other men have pre-arranged that we shall see and think and feel.

We must not, however, push our biological metaphors too far. Society is not an organism in the same sense in which a man's body is an organism. In the latter the biological units exist only for the sake of the body as a whole; they have no separate interests, and no separate consciousness at all. In the former the units are individuals having reason and will. In thought, at anyrate, their interests may be dissociated, and are constantly dissociated from those of the body. The only consciousness at all is the individual consciousness; the favourite phrases of the evolutionist writers, common consciousness, social consciousness, tribal conscience, are unabashed metaphors. The well-being of society, therefore, has no conscious existence except as reflected in the minds of the individuals who compose it. The individual person has a reality as real as, and indeed more real than any other thing or object in the universe whatever, and no employment of imperfect biological analogies must be allowed to obscure this central fact.

Nevertheless, given the individual, however he may have arrived at self-dom, duty has a meaning for him apart from society. He can, at any rate in abstract thought, separate his interests and efficiency from those of other men. "Why should I sacrifice myself for others?" is so far from being an impossible or irrational question, that when the individual rises to a certain stage of self-consciousness it is bound to be asked. An adequate account of morality may only be possible from the social point of view, but the individual point of view is the first and most natural one.

The egoistic hedonist regards his duties to self as ultimate; the utilitarian regards them as of equal importance with those which he owes to his neighbour. And one of these two positions seems the natural position of orthodox Christian Ethics. I must do right because of my own future happiness, or because of the duty of self-culture on the one hand; or because I am bound to consider the happiness or perfection of others as well as my own. Traditional Christian Ethics has never insisted that I must do right simply and solely for the sake of others.

We cannot indeed in a strict sense have rights against society, since the very idea of right is relative to social law. The social contract is a hypothesis which depends on the still less justifiable assumption of an individual existing apart from society, and having rights apart from society. Hence we may not speak of society and the individual as joint owners or partners having equal claims over the individual's life. My position with regard to society is one of mere duty.

A somewhat important distinction can be drawn between the virtues which are primarily due to intellect and negative will (control), and those which are primarily due to emotion and impulse. To the former class belong prudence, temperance, justice; to the latter benevolence, purity, courage. Many virtues present a very different aspect according as they are due primarily to principle, or primarily to impulse. Thus there is a marked difference between temperance and purity, cool fortitude and dashing courage, exactness of statement and passionate desire for truth. Writers and schools lay different stress on the two groups of virtues. The Stoics, Kant and Butler, lay chief emphasis on excellences of principle; the Shaftesbury and the Utilitarian on the excellence arising from good impulse. But all schools necessarily recognize both in some degree. All agree that the virtuous man knows what is right (wisdom); that he knows what is due to others and desires to give it (justice). He has proper regard for the pleasures and pains of others (benevolence), while he has not too much regard for his own pains (courage), or his own pleasures (temperance).

In different ages and stages of development different ideals of virtue have predominated, while not absolutely obliterating the rival ideals. The supreme virtue with the ancients was self-culture; with the early Christians, purity and self-denial. In the middle ages the veneration for courage and fidelity gives us the ideal of chivalry; the architectonic virtue in the eighteenth century is prudence. The sexes vary in the importance they attach to purity and candour, courage and pity; so do different ages—the boy, the middle-aged, and the old; so do different nations.

The smallest number of virtues which we can recognize as generic would seem to be six, viz., prudence, courage, temperance, justice, truthfulness, and benevolence.

§ 4. Prudence.

Prudence is used for (1) practical wisdom in the widest sense, and (2) practical wisdom directed to the advantage of self. Note that for the mass of people in the middle classes, prudence in the narrower sense is still the supreme virtue. And generally speaking, it is true that we lay stress on the rational virtues. Generosity, hospitality, reckless courage, are the excellences of an earlier stage of civilization; to-day we chiefly admire justice, sobriety, self-restraint in face of danger.

To some extent the ethical method we accept will help to determine what place we shall allot to prudence. Pure altruism places "wisdom for a man's self," as Bacon calls it, outside the rank of primary virtues, while allowing it a secondary and auxiliary position—since I can only be serviceable to others on condition that I pay some attention to my own welfare. Pure egoism makes prudence the architectonic virtue. Utilitarianism places it in a position alongside of benevolence; my happiness counts for one as well as yours.

Prudence in the widest sense is "a conscious habit of correct thinking on matters of action" (Aristotle, "Nic. Eth.," VI. v.). It involves right choice of ends, and right choice of means. It guarantees both premises of the ethical syllogism and draws the conclusion. It differs from merely speculative knowledge, since it deals with affairs of practice, which it knows concretely in all their details, and not abstractly in propositions. These complex affairs of actual life can only be known by experience, and natural tact is necessary as well. The prudent man necessarily acts from reason and not mere impulse. Hence, other things equal, we must take time before acting (caution), and we must have self-control or firmness, intelligence, and knowledge from which to reason. Hence the obstacles to prudence are haste, strength of feeling, weakness of reason, and want of knowledge. In excess caution becomes hesitation, and firmness becomes obstinacy.

As Aristotle points out, there is a reaction of our general moral condition on our practical intelligence.[1] An effective knowledge of what is really worth striving for is impossible to the vicious man; and in some forms of vice—those which imply loss of self-control—the man is ignorant of the minor premise in the ethical syllogism. The angry man often denies that he is angry, the excessive drinker does not realize where excess begins.

"Faults in the life breed errors in the brain."

[1] Cf. Nic. Eth. VI. v., xii.; VII. iii.

§ 5. Courage.

Courage is obviously not adequately defined by reference to principle. It is a virtue of impulse, and cannot be resolved into knowledge of what ought to be feared. It implies fearlessness in the face of what may be rationally feared, as well as in the face of what should not. A defect of emotional energy, of combativeness, of strong desires, can only in part be overcome by reflection. And this secondary courage has not the æsthetic attraction of the impulsive sort. It has sometimes been thought that in the progress of modern society, the decay of militarism, and the scientific aspect given even to war itself, less room would be left for this virtue, and that men will learn to do comfortably without it, as well as without hair and teeth. But this is hardly probable. The establishment of socialistic utopias is perhaps less likely to bring peace than a sword; and in any event in colonizing savage parts of the world, room will still be found for impulsive courage when it is banished from the paternal industrialism of civilization.

§ 6. Temperance.

In its full conception self-control is not to be restricted to the bodily appetites and the pleasures of touch and taste. Other desires, and the emotions and sentiments, come within the scope of it. Dante places lust, gluttony, avarice, and prodigality, wrath and melancholy, together as sins of incontinence. Gush, talkativeness, and self-assertion are as much offences against temperance as drunkenness. In Aristotle's discussion of this virtue the doctrine of the mean does not occupy a prominent place. Of the two extremes, self-indulgence and unnatural insensibility, only the former exists, the latter is theoretical. But Aristotle knew nothing of the asceticism of the East; and to him the Christian practice of chastity would have seemed as truly intemperate as excess.

§ 7. Justice.

Professor Sidgwick has analysed with great subtlety the common notion of justice.[1] He points out the following elements:

(1) Mere impartiality, *i.e.* absence of irrationality in distribution.

(2) Reparation for injury.

(3) Conservative justice, or observance of those relations determined by law and custom which regulate the greater part of our conduct towards others; *i.e.* (i) observance of laws, and of contracts or definite understandings; (ii) fulfilment of natural and normal expectations.

(4) Ideal justice, or the distribution of things in accordance with what we believe to be fair and right, even when there are no laws or definite understandings to guide us.

---

[1] "Meth. of Ethics," book iii. ch. v.

"Mere justice" implies a reference to this ideal. Equity in law had its origin in an attempt to get at a higher form of justice than mere justice. It gave relief to those who were wronged, yet had no legal remedy. In applying abstract laws to particular cases, injustice may result. It is the duty of the judge to prevent this. Yet the courts of equity must be governed by precedent, otherwise greater hardships will occur. And so a system of rigid but, on the whole, fairer law grows up, under the name of equity. Of the immense service done to humanity by the Roman courts of equity, out of whose decisions the majestic fabric of the civil law arose, this is not the place to speak.

What determines the ideals? The production (as geometers say) of the principles of justice which we already recognize, further than the common sense of society has yet carried them.

How difficult this may be is seen in the discussion of such a question as "fair wages." What are fair wages? Two or three answers may be given:

(1) Wages determined by free competition. Something between the highest the master can normally give, and the lowest the workman will normally take.

(2) Wages determined by the needs of the workman. But does this include the present or some higher (and from a moral point of view more desirable) standard of comfort? And if it can be shown that the maintenance of an industry is impossible except

N

on starvation wages, shall we sacrifice the ζῆν to the εὖ ζῆν, as some trades unions seem to wish?[1]

(3) Wages determined by the merits of the workman. It seems impossible in such cases to reconcile the competing ideals.

Justice then involves reference to some standard,—one already recognized or one which ought to be recognized. There is no doubt a great danger in subordinating the former to the latter, to disobey laws and to break contracts in obedience to ideals which are usually intangible, and frequently arbitrary and impossible. On the other hand, such substitution of ideal for conservative justice is sometimes the condition of moral advance.

[1] Is there a right to live, and, if so, does it include the right to produce a dozen children?

CHAPTER VIII.

ETHICS IN RELATION TO THEOLOGY AND LAW.

§ 1. Ethics and Theology.

THE relations of Ethics and Theology are somewhat complicated. Ethics supplies arguments for the existence of God, and means of determining His attributes. Theologians tell us it is man's duty to seek God, and to believe in Him. This assumes that duty can exist and can be known prior to the acceptance of any form of religion. They apply to God certain ethical predicates; He is just, true, merciful, jealous, and so on. These terms must have a meaning apart from any theological implications. Christian teachers argue that the claim of Christianity to a Divine origin is proved by its exalted morality, which again assumes that ethical ideas are *nobis notiora*.

On the other hand Theology supplies special features: (1) in the form, and (2) in the content of morality. Theological study naturally leads to the acceptance of a jural form of Ethics. The Ten Commandments are a code of laws, and the more stringent demands of Christian morality take the form of glosses and interpretations of these, or that of supplementary laws. Morality is imposed on us by a command of God; and obedience is exacted by means of sanctions, pleasures and pains in this life or the next.

This view, though the most obvious and the most widely spread amongst Christians, was not the only possible one. Thoughtful men soon saw that the obligations of morality could not be entirely, or even chiefly, ascribed to the will of God, and the sanctions with which that will was enforced. It must in some way be determined by the divine nature itself. God is absolute Goodness, and man must desire God for this reason; Morality is no longer obedience to God's Law, but an effort to become like God, and to enter into the completest possible relation to Him.

This more idealistic view is supported by the doctrine of Sin, which has its origin in the ceremonialism and legalism of the priestly code, but is greatly developed by the prophets and by Christian theologians. Evil doing is looked on not only as the breach of a law, but as a personal defilement. Sin comes to be thought of as having a certain substantiality of its own, in antithesis to God.

In the content or matter of morality Theology has introduced the conception of duties to God as a separate kind of right conduct. It has given us the theological virtues, faith, hope, and love, and laid an especial stress on purity as opposed to mere temperance; it has given a much more important place to patience and humility.[1]

[1] See chap. vii., § 2, above.

In the same way it has made the conception of right conduct more strict. It has quickened sympathy and conscience, and thus led to more and more lofty ideals. It has insisted on the positive side of virtue, and on the importance of the Good Will as opposed to particular external compliances with law. Morality instead of being a sum of excellences having different sources, is constituted essentially from within by the will to comply with God's Law, or to be like Him.

Finally, Theology gives us a new motive to virtue, in the love of God. Christianity especially emphasizes the obligations of love and gratitude to the incarnate and crucified Son of God.

§ 2. Morality and Law.

Law consists of a set of rules enforced by Government either directly or indirectly. Many of these rules are also supported by the social sanction. Positive Morality may be regarded as a set of rules enforced by the social sanction; but there is a somewhat undetermined area, where the social sanction ceases to be definite, which yet belongs to the sphere of moral conduct. The acts enforced by both Law and the social sanction belong chiefly to the sphere of extra-regarding action—*i.e.*, to justice and benevolence. Even here the social sanction is much more effective in the case of the normal individual because (1) more speedy, (2) more flexible and adaptable, (3) more continuous and (4) more certain. But Morality covers a much wider area than Law. Law can only aim at repressing or producing external acts; Morality can go farther and aim at producing or repressing elements of feeling and thought, *i.e.*, character. It deals with intention and motive.

Ethics deals with conduct viewed without special reference to external codes. Jurisprudence deals with the codes enforced by the political organs of society. The actual content of Law is often, and indeed always, imperfectly moral; because Law can only take account of such elements of conduct as are amenable to political treatment. We cannot have definite evidence of motives, or other states of consciousness; and external punishments cannot be relied on to alter them. The conduct which I believe to be best may be in advance of that which Law orders, though of the same kind; or it may be at variance with Law.

Morality follows Law in so far as Morality enforces obedience to laws already made. It goes further, and "clothes the bare skeleton of law;" it "regulates actions in conformity with the relations which actual law has introduced." And as Morality largely consists in ideally perfecting these relations it prepares the way for fresh legislation, and regulates the making of new rules. Thus the interaction of Law and Morality is twofold. To the young, and the morally backward, Law serves as a moral code; the good transcend this code; as society improves, acts which were left to the operation of the social sanction are gradually brought into the sphere of legal punishment, and a man is compelled to do to-day what a century ago was regarded as an act of more than ordinary virtue.

An important distinction exists between Law and Morality in regard to merit. Law seldom rewards; its sanctions are almost exclusively painful. Positive Morality rewards as well as punishes. Those evil acts which are punished both by the civil magistrate and by public opinion are *crimes;* those which are not punished by the former but only by the latter are often called *vices,* though this usage of the word is not always strictly observed. There is thus nothing exactly answering on the side of virtue to the term crime: that is, there are no acts which the State habitually and regularly rewards as a matter of course. Special honours and gifts to successful soldiers or to brave firemen and other heroes in civil life are not awarded with sufficient regularity and certainty to constitute an exception; nor are they awarded by the regular State tribunals acting as such. The virtues of temperance, justice, prudence, and benevolence are seldom if ever considered as deserving or requiring recognition by the State. The religious and social sanctions are usually sufficient to secure a fair average degree of excellence in these aspects of conduct.

§ 3. Obedience to Law.

Is it ever right to disobey the Law? From the Utilitarian point of view the question must be solved by a consideration of the relative advantages and disadvantages of disobedience to an unjust law. Setting aside the direct personal consequences to ourselves and those who imitate us, that is, the legal punishment we incur, we see that all disobedience involves the further evil of weakening the respect for Law and the habit of obedience in ourselves and others; it brings society, as Hobbes urged, a step nearer anarchy. On the other hand the conditions of our act may be such that this danger may be reduced to a minimum; our act may be known only to a few, or the line we purpose to follow may be quite unlikely to commend itself to persons of a lawless character. These conditions, however, seldom obtain, and the Utilitarian will feel that the balance of advantage in favour of disobedience must be very decided to justify resort to it. Nevertheless when there is a decided opposition between positive Morality and Law, and the collective conscience is more likely to be scandalized by obedience than by disobedience, he may feel that the risk is worth running, and he may hope that his disobedience and the punishment which it brings on him may incidentally lead to a change in the Law.

The Intuitionist, especially if he regards conscience as a divinely given and inspired guide will necessarily assert that its dicta are absolutely binding even in opposition to Law and positive Morality. But he will remember that Law is on the whole the outcome of the conscience of the community, that to prefer his own moral perceptions when in opposition to those of others is dangerous, because self-love and other still more subtle emotions may easily bias his judgment without being recognized and discounted. If his conviction of the duty of disobedience is not of the strongest he will be influenced by the same kind of comparison of relative disadvantages as the Utilitarians. If he feels overwhelmingly certain of the duty of disobedience he will disobey, no matter at what cost. Thus the chance of conflict is greater in his case. It is this occasionally anti-legal tendency of the intuitional and theological Ethics which leads Hobbes to call the doctrine, that "whatever a man does against his conscience is sin," a "doctrine subversive of civil society."[1]

§ 4. Casuistry.

In the systematization of morality, casuistry has borne an important part. Growing up as a consequence of the penitential system of the Catholic Church, it has its justification in the jural view of morality. If moral truths are expressed as a system of laws, we must assume that they are continuous and consistent. The application of these laws to particular cases of difficulty which either do not appear to fall under any rule, or else appear to fall under two or more conflicting rules, is the object of the science of casuistry.[2] Such " cases of con-

[1] "Leviathan," Part I., chap. xxix.
[2] "Cases of conscience are those in which conflicting duties and conflicting rules are weighed deliberately, the time and

science" had of course constantly occurred, but when private confession became frequent, regular, and compulsory, need was felt for authoritative and systematic treatment of them. Many of the great thirteenth and fourteenth-century theologians wrote books on moral theology; and different schools gradually developed, some leaning towards rigorism and others taking wider and less exacting views. The dislike of Protestants and liberal Roman Catholics to the system of casuistry is due to (1) its connection with the practice of compulsory confession and of "direction," in which the individual gives up the control of his conduct more or less entirely to the guidance of an expert;[1] (2) its substitution of a formal obedience to rule for a living effort after the best possible conduct. If it be true that only *that* conduct is good for me which I believe to be right in my own conscience, mere acceptance of the rules of morality cannot be morality; mere material rightness is not rightness at all (chap. iii. § 2). On the other hand, it must be remembered that mere formal rightness will not do. We want to know our duty; and we cannot, even

circumstances allowing of this. Cases of necessity are those in which a man is compelled to violate common duties and common rules by the pressure of extreme danger or fear." Whewell, "Elements of Morality," bk. iii., chap. xv.

[1] The revolt against theological experts was one of the central features of the Reformation. With a translation of the Bible in his hand, and the grace of God in his heart, there was nothing worth knowing which the ordinary man thought he could not know for himself.

with the most perfect honesty of purpose, always tell what it is. (3) The connection of casuistry with the special Jesuit doctrine of Probabilism (see Sidgwick, "Hist.," p. 153, 2nd edit.), with which, however, it has no necessary association. (4) The danger to morality of minute inquiry into the limits and qualification of moral rules. This danger of course may be very real; but unless ethics is to become a mere aggregate of vague generalities and stimulating appeals to emotion, the danger must be faced. The study of moral pathology, it may be said, is not *virginibus puerisque*, but for priests and philosophers.

Appeals have been made of late from the side of orthodox utilitarianism for a new casuistry, and it may be hoped that for the benefit of those who still normally think of morality as law, the attempt may be made to supply the want.

CHAPTER IX.

BRIEF SKETCH OF ENGLISH ETHICAL THEORIES.

§ 1. Hobbes and his Opponents.

HOBBES (1588-1679) taught that the real end for each to seek is his own good—that is, his own pleasure or means of pleasure—his self-preservation. Hence the natural state of mankind is *war*. But this Egoism is self-limiting; a kind of compact, or treaty of peace, is entered into—the result of selfishness and fear. Thus arise Society and the State. Since any settled social order is better than the state of nature, a good man will always obey the laws of the State, for fear of weakening the social order. For the same reasons a strong government is needed; and thus we are led to the peculiar absolutism supported by Hobbes. What the sovereign commands is right; what he forbids is wrong. If there were no law there would be no justice, no distinction of *meum* and *tuum*. At the same time it is reasonable for me to obey moral rules only as long as others obey them; hence, again, the necessity for a strong government. Thus the system of Hobbes was essentially egoistic.

Hobbes's system aroused great opposition. Attacks

were made on it from two sides. It was not denied by one set of writers, that happiness, well-being, etc., were the proper aim and end of action; only they urged that the good at which we ought to aim is the *general* good as distinguished from the good of the agent himself, the "common good of all rationals" (*Cumberland*), the "good of the public" (*Shaftesbury*). This line of argument gradually led to Utilitarianism, as good came to be more and more clearly identified with pleasure. Other writers, however, approached the question from a wholly different point of view, and assimilated the rules of morality to the propositions of mathematics; they were truths which could be deduced from the very nature of man, the world, and God. There are, says Clarke (1675-1729), in "Morals, as in Geometry, certain unalterable relations, aspects and proportions of things, with their consequent agreements and disagreements." No one will deny this, and refuse to see the truth of moral axioms, unless from "the extremest stupidity of mind, corruption of manners, and perverseness of spirit." For men to act wrongly and wickedly is to act "contrary to that understanding, reason, and judgment, which God has implanted in their nature, on purpose to enable them to discern the difference between good and evil. 'Tis attempting to destroy that order by which the universe subsists." To this Rational or Intuitive school of Ethics belonged Cudworth (1617-1688), another opponent of Hobbes, as well as Clarke. Locke (1632-1704) also puts forward an intuitionist theory; but he held that the reason for moral conduct lay outside the standard itself, in the pleasure and pain which obedience and disobedience respectively caused us.

§ 2. Shaftesbury and Butler.

Shaftesbury (1671-1719) is the predecessor to whom Butler is most indebted. The general view of Ethics taken by him was much influenced by Greek thought. Nothing is absolutely ill except what is absolutely detrimental to the whole system to which it belongs; hence even "private self-affection" is good, except when it militates against the good of the species, which only happens when it is too strong. We have a "reflex affection," that is, we reflect on our own affections (impulses), and approve or disapprove them. A creature which has this "reflecting faculty" invariably approves what is right and disapproves what is wrong. It is this reflex goodness which constitutes Virtue: Shaftesbury calls it the " Sense of Right and Wrong."

Good actions done from fear and hope, that is, from egoistic reasons, are not virtuous ; even if the object of the fear or hope be God. As soon as any one "is come to have any affection toward what is morally good, and can like or affect such good for its own sake, as good and amiable in itself ; then he is in some degree virtuous, and not till then." Shaftesbury divides the impulses into (1) Natural or kindly affections, leading to the "good of the Public ;" (2) Self-affections, leading to the " good of the Private ;" and (3) Unnatural affections, contrary to all good. And he lays down, that to have the natural affections strong is to "have the chief means and power of self-enjoyment," and " to want them is certain misery;" that to have the self-affections too strong, or "beyond their degree of subordinacy" to the natural affections is also miserable; and that to have the unnatural affections is to be miserable in the highest degree. We thus see Shaftesbury laying down the " hierarchy of impulses," on which Butler afterwards built his system.

Butler (1692-1752) in some degree combined the lines of argument adopted against Hobbes by Shaftesbury and by Clarke. He tells us " that there are two ways in which the subject of morals may be treated. One begins from inquiring into the abstract relations of things [Clarke, etc.]: the other from a matter of fact, namely, what the particular nature of man is, its several parts, their economy or constitution; from whence it proceeds to determine what course of life it is which is correspondent to this whole nature [Shaftesbury]. In the former method the conclusion is expressed thus: that vice is contrary to the nature and reason of things, in the latter, that it is a violation or breaking in upon our own nature. They both lead us to the same thing, our obligations to the practice of virtue; and thus they exceedingly strengthen and enforce each other. . . . The following discourses [Butler's own Sermons] proceed chiefly in this latter method." Butler points out that in human nature there are two supreme impulses —self-love and conscience. He lays stress on the disinterestedness of our benevolent impulses; and shows that in all our desires except self-love itself, the primary end, the object desired, is not our own pleasure but some external thing, *i.e.*, they are extra-regarding. The two principles, Self-love and Conscience (= Moral Sentiment), preside over these inferior impulses; but Butler does not quite clearly determine the relative positions of self-love and conscience with regard to each other, whether they are strictly co-ordinate, or one of them subordinate to the other. On the whole, however, Butler seems to give the supremacy to conscience; which is the guide assigned to us by the Author of Nature. "Every man is naturally a law to himself;" or in other words, "every one may find within himself the rule of right and obligations to follow it." We arrive, then, at a conception of man as a Hierarchy of impulses, conscience being supreme. No man can "be said to act conformably to his constitution of nature unless he allows to that superior principle the absolute authority which is due to it." "You cannot form a notion of this faculty, conscience, without taking in judgment, direction, superintendency. This is a constituent part of the idea. . . . Had it strength as it had right; had it power as it had manifest authority, it would absolutely govern the world."

§ 3. Hutcheson, Hume, and Smith.

Hutcheson (1694-1747) went still further. He showed that the happiness derived from the kindly affections does not prevent them from being really disinterested. The good man is benevolent for other reasons than that of the pleasure which he gains from benevolence. There is a natural sense which recognizes by "an immediate and undefinable intuition" what is good in our affections and approves of them in consequence; while it disapproves of those that are base and unworthy. Hutcheson sets himself to prove " (1) that some actions have to men an immediate goodness; or that by a supreme sense, which I call a moral one, we have pleasure in the contemplation of such actions in others, and are determined to love the agent (and much more do we perceive pleasure in being conscious of having done such actions ourselves), without any view of further natural advantage from them. (2) That what excites us to these actions, which we call virtuous, is not an intention to obtain even this sensible pleasure; much less the future rewards from sanctions of laws, or any other natural good, which may be the consequence of the virtuous action; but an entirely different principle of action from interest or self-love." Hutcheson "definitely identified virtue with benevolence."

The doctrine of a Moral Sense, originated by Shaftesbury and Hutcheson, is accepted by Hume (1711-1776), and developed by him, while an intellectual element is more explicitly admitted. "I am apt to suspect that *reason* and *sentiment* concur in almost all moral determinations and conclusions. It is probable . . . that this final sentence depends on some internal sense or feeling"; but to appreciate or discover moral beauty, like beauty in art, apparently "demands the assistance of our intellectual faculties." But what it approves is no longer mere undefined " goodness," but pleasure, either for oneself or others. It is thus that Hume may be regarded as in some sense the founder of modern Utilitarianism. His attitude, however, is rather that of the psychologist than the moralist. He analyses our moral ideas and finds the character of utility in all kinds of virtuous conduct.

Adam Smith (1723-1790) agrees with Hume that the quality of utility will be universally found in the objects of moral approbation. But the utility is not the cause of the approbation. "We either approve or disapprove of our own conduct according as we feel that, when we place ourselves in the situation of another man, and view it, as it were, with his eyes, and from his station, we either can or cannot entirely enter into and sympathize with the sentiments and motives which influence it." Thus the moral sense is analysed into a kind of complex sympathy. By seeing what kinds of conduct are universally approved of by the moral sense, we can lay down rules of conduct, general moral principles.

§ 4. Paley, Bentham, and Mill.

Paley (1743-1805) defines Virtue as "the doing good to mankind, in obedience to the will of God, and for the sake of everlasting happiness." He thus resolves all virtue into benevolence, which is (roughly speaking) the utilitarian point of view, but introduces an egoistic element, since virtue is to be done for the sake of *our own* ultimate happiness. He overlooks the fact that many virtuous actions are, and have been, done without any reference to God's will or a future life, as by atheists. And he is only on the verge of Utilitarianism, since he does not resolve *good* into *pleasure;* indeed, he expressly excludes pleasures of sense from his idea of happiness. He lays great stress on the social affections and on the pleasures of action. But his general system is little affected by this; he seems to drop out of sight this arbitrary definition of happiness; and in the working out of his principles he is perhaps more consistently Hedonistic than any of his predecessors. Paley was a Conservative Utilitarian; it was his object to show that the current morality was thoroughly justifiable from the utilitarian point of view.

On the other hand, Bentham (1748-1832) was a Radical Utilitarian, whose object was to criticise and reconstruct Ethics and Jurisprudence from the utilitarian point of view. Bentham was the first to make Utilitarianism quite definite, by identifying good and happiness with pleasure, and by getting clear of the older egoistic view.[1] He laid down that (1) Actions are right according as they conduce to the general happiness—*i.e.*, to the greatest happiness of the greatest number. (2) By Happiness we mean Pleasure. (3) This must be the *sole* test of rightness and wrongness; we must not admit any rival principle even for a moment. (4) We must allow the possibility of some kind of "Moral Arithmetic," by which we can compare the amount of happiness produced by different kinds of actions. These propositions Bentham stated, and supported, with great precision and effect. He eliminated the theological element which hampered Paley; and, in working out the details of his system, was hindered by no tenderness for existing beliefs or institutions. He based his ethical theory on a full and careful psychological investigation; since his "moral arithmetic" demanded exactitude and completeness in his review of the sources and effects of different kinds of feeling.

J. S. Mill (1806-1873) was a disciple of Bentham. He popularized the doctrines of his master and did a great deal towards rendering them less offensive to outsiders. While Bentham never sought to conciliate orthodoxy by compromise, Mill was always ready to explain and extenuate. The only points to which it

---

[1] But even in Bentham we discover some purely egoistic elements. For instance, he says the object of Deontology (*i.e.*, Ethics) is "to instruct the inquirer in the management of the affections so that they may be made most subservient to his own well-being." ("Deontology," vol. ii., p. 27; cf. vol. i., p. 18.)

is here necessary to allude are: (1) His attempt to distinguish quality (kind) as well as quantity (degree) in pleasures; and (2) His attempt to exhibit more clearly the connection between justice and the principle of utility. The former has been already alluded to; the best recent writers on Utilitarianism, Professor Grote (an intuitionist) and Mr. Sidgwick (an utilitarian), consider it subversive of the possibility of that "moral arithmetic" which Utilitarianism pre-supposes. The latter attempt is a psychological account of the various sentiments and notions which cluster round the conception of justice in the minds of ordinary people, rather than an ethical analysis of what, on utilitarian principles, this idea of justice involves.

Mill considers that the central core of the idea of justice is *law*. He sees in justice two main elements, the principle of utility, and a sentiment, viz., the desire that punishment should overtake those who infringe the principle. This sentiment is *moralized* by being in subordination to the principle of utility; in itself it is non-moral, being simply "the animal desire to repel or retaliate a hurt or damage to oneself, or to those with whom one sympathizes, widened so as to include all persons, by the human capacity of enlarged sympathy and the human conception of intelligent self-interest" ("Utilitarianism," p. 79). It has been usual to represent Revenge as a perversion of the desire for justice; but Mill reverses this order, and explains justice by revenge.

§ 5. Tabular view of English ethical theories up to Mill.

Intuitionist
- 1. The motive for doing the right action lies in the intuition itself. — Clarke, Cudworth, Hutcheson
- 2. The motive is my own happiness. — Locke

Utilitarian
- 1. The motive for doing the right action lies in the fact that it tends to the greatest happiness of all. — Bentham, Mill
- 2. The motive is my own happiness. — Paley

Egoistic . . . . Hobbes

The Intuitionists are divided on the (psychological) question as to the nature of the Intuitive faculty:—

1. The Intuitive faculty is of the nature of a sense (cf. Sense of Beauty). — Shaftesbury, Hutcheson
2. It is equivalent to Moral Reason . — Clarke, Locke

To Hobbes replied:—

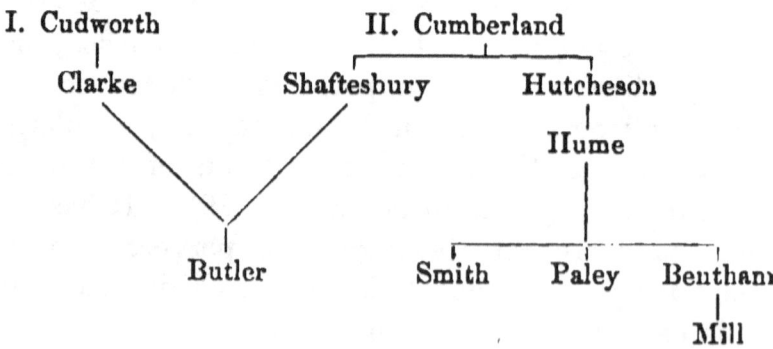

APPENDIX A.

BOOKS RECOMMENDED.

GENERAL.

Alexander, " Moral Order and Progress."
Gizycki and Coit, " Student's Manual of Ethical Philosophy."
Green, " Prolegomena to Ethics."
Lotze, " Practical Philosophy," edited by Ladd.
Martineau, " Types of Ethical Theory," especially vol. ii.
Muirhead, " Elements of Ethics."
Sidgwick, " Methods of Ethics."
Spencer, " Principles of Ethics."
Stephen, " Science of Ethics."
Wilson and Fowler, " Principles of Morals," especially vol. ii.

CHAPTER I.

THE SCOPE AND METHOD OF ETHICS.

Sidgwick, " Methods of Ethics," Bk. I., ch. i., vi.
    ,,   " History of Ethics," ch. i.

Muirhead, "Elements of Ethics," Bk. I.; Bk. II., ch. i.
Alexander, "Moral Order and Progress," Introduction; Bk. I., ch. ii.
Stephen, "Science of Ethics," ch. i.
Spencer, "Principles of Ethics," Part. I. ("Data"), ch. xi.-xv.
Green, "Prolegomena to Ethics," Introduction.
Martineau, "Types of Ethical Theory," vol. ii., pp. 1-64.
Aristotle, "Nic. Eth.," Bk. I.
Balfour, in "Mind," vol. iii., pp. 67 *seq.*, 276 *seq.*

CHAPTER II.

GOOD, HAPPINESS, PLEASURE.

On Good.

    Sidgwick, "Methods," Bk. I., ch. ix.; Bk. III., ch. xiv.
    Muirhead, "Elements," Bk. IV.
    Gizycki and Coit, "Student's Manual," pp. 6 *seq.*
    Green, "Prolegomena," pp. 178 *seq.*, pp. 399-415.

On Pleasure and Happiness as an End.

    Sidgwick, as above.
    Muirhead, "Elements," Bk. III.
    Grote, "Moral Ideals," ch. xii.-xiii.

Green, "Prolegomena to Ethics," Bk. III., ch. iv.;
Bk. IV., ch. iv.
Alexander, "Moral Order," pp. 196 *seq.*
Pater, "Renaissance," *ad fin.*
Bradley, "Ethical Studies," Essay III.

On Perfection as an End.

Alexander, "Moral Order," pp. 187 *seq.*
Green, "Prolegomena," Bk. IV., ch. iv.

On Social Health or Vitality as an End.

Stephen, "Science of Ethics," pp. 137 *seq.*
Alexander, "Moral Order," pp. 233 *seq.*
Articles in "Mind," vol. i., pp. 52 *seq.*, 334 *seq.*;
vol. xv., pp. 342 *seq.*

On Humanity as an End.

Kant, "Metaphysic of Ethics."
Bridges, "General View of Positivism," pp. 67 *seq.*
Green, "Prolegomena," pp. 189-201.

CHAPTER III.

On Right and Rights.

Calderwood, "Handbook of Moral Philosophy,"
Part I., Div. I., ch. vi.
Austin, "Lectures on Jurisprudence," vol. i., pp. 293 *seq.*, 353 *seq.*

Sidgwick, " Methods," Bk. i., ch. iii.
Alexander, " Moral Order," pp. 27 *seq.*, 142 *seq.*
Fowler, " Principles of Morals," Part II., pp. 140 *seq.*

On Natural Rights, Law of Nature.

Butler, " Sermons on Human Nature."
Maine, " Ancient Law," ch. iii.-iv.
Sidgwick, " Methods," Bk. I., ch. vi., § 2.
Stephen, " Science of Ethics," ch. iv.

On Duty and Obligation.

Calderwood, Part I., Div. I., ch. v.; Div. II., ch. iv.
Grote, " Moral Ideals," ch. vii.
Alexander, " Moral Order," pp. 142 *seq.*
Spencer, " Principles of Morality," Part I. (" Data "), ch. vii.
Austin, " Lectures on Jurisprudence," vol. i., pp. 91 *seq.*
Bradley, " Ethical Studies," Essay IV.

On Merit.

Stephen, " Science of Ethics," pp. 264-277.
Gizycki and Coit, pp. 103 *seq.*
Martineau, " Types of Ethical Theory," vol. ii., pp. 75 *seq.*

On Responsibility.

    Alexander, " Moral Order," pp. 31 *seq.*, 333 *seq.*
    Gizycki and Coit, pp. 174 *seq.*
    Bradley, " Ethical Studies," Essay I.

CHAPTER IV.

HEDONISTIC THEORIES.

    Sidgwick, " Methods," Bk. II. and Bk. IV.
        ,,   " History," *sub voc.* Cumberland, Hume, Paley, Bentham, Mill.
    Muirhead, " Elements," Bk. III., ch. i.
    Alexander, " Moral Order," pp. 196-232.
    Mill, " Utilitarianism."
    Bentham, "Principles of Morals and Legislation," ch. i.
    Bentham, " Deontology."
    Green, "Prolegomena," Bk. iii., ch. iv., pp. 233-255; Bk. IV., ch. iii., iv.
    Martineau, " Types of Ethical Theory," vol. ii., pp. 283 *seq.*

On Egoism and Altruism.

    Bradley, " Ethical Studies," Essay VII.
    Stephen, " Science of Ethics," ch. vi.
    Spencer, "Principles of Ethics," Pt. I. (" Data of Ethics ").
    Bentham, " Deontology," vol. i.

On Evolution theory of Ethics.

>   Stephen, " Science of Ethics," ch. ix.
>   Muirhead, " Elements," Bk. III., ch. iii.
>   Sidgwick, " History," pp. 244-248.
>   Martineau, " Types of Ethical Theory," vol. ii., pp. 335 *seq.*
>   Bradley, " Ethical Studies," Essay V.-VI.

CHAPTER V.

INTUITIONAL THEORIES.

>   Sidgwick, " Methods," Bk. I., ch. viii. ; Bk. III.
>   ,,   " History," *sub voc.* Clarke, Butler, Hutcheson, etc.
>   Butler, " Sermons on Human Nature."
>   Dugald Stewart, " Outlines of Moral Philosophy."
>   Calderwood, "Handbook," Part I., Div. I.
>   Muirhead, " Elements," Bk. II., ch. ii.
>   Martineau, " Types of Ethical Theory," vol. ii.

On the Æsthetic view.

>   Stephen, " Science of Ethics," pp. 332 *seq.*

On Kant's theory.

>   Kant, " Metaphysic of Morals," translated by Abbott.

Caird, "Philosophy of Kant," vol. ii., pp. 143, 405.
Green, "Phil. Works," vol. ii., pp. 83 *seq.*
See also Ueberweg or Erdmann, *sub voc.* Kant.

CHAPTER VI.

THE PSYCHOLOGY OF ETHICS.

On Moral Reason.

Sidgwick, "Methods," Bk. I., ch. iii.
Alexander, "Moral Order," pp. 102 *seq.*
Stephen, "Science of Ethics," pp. 58 *seq.*
Martineau, "Types of Ethical Theory," vol. ii., pp. 92 *seq.*
Stewart, "Active and Moral Powers," Bk. II., chap. v.
Fowler, "Principles of Morals," Part II., ch. vii.

On Moral Emotion.

Höffding, "Psychology" (transl.), p. 259 *seq.*
Sully, "Human Mind," vol. ii., pp. 135 *seq.*
Stephen, "Science of Ethics," ch. viii.
Stewart, "Active and Moral Powers," Bks. I. and II.
Martineau, "Types of Ethical Theory," vol. ii., pp. 257 *seq.*
Fowler, "Principles of Morals," Pt. II., ch. i.-v.

On Pleasure and Desire.

> Ward, art. "Psychology" in the "Encyclopædia Britannica," p. 74.
> Sully, "Human Mind," vol. ii., pp. 203 *seq.*
> James, "Principles of Psychology," vol. ii., pp. 549 *seq.*
> Sidgwick, "Methods," Bk. I., ch. iv.
> Green, "Prolegomena," Bk. II., ch. ii.; Bk. III., ch. i., pp. 163-177.

On Freedom of the Will.

> Sully, "Human Mind," vol. ii., pp. 292 *seq.*, 364 *seq.*
> James, "Principles of Psychology," vol. ii., pp. 569 *seq.*
> Stephen, "Science of Ethics," pp. 278 *seq.*
> Caird, "Philosophy of Kant," vol. ii., pp. 241 *seq.*
> Sidgwick, "Methods," Bk. I., ch. v.
> Mill, "Examination of Hamilton," ch. xxvi.
> Fowler, "Principles of Morals," Part II., ch. ix.
> Alexander, "Moral Order," pp. 336 *seq.*
> Green, "Prolegomena," pp. 79 *seq.*; and Bk. II.
> Schopenhauer, "The World as Will and Idea" (trans.), vol. i., pp. 349 *seq.*

On Habit.

> Sully, "Human Mind," vol. ii., pp. 224 *seq.*, 280 *seq.*

James, "Principles of Psychology," vol. i., pp. 104 *seq.*; vol. ii., pp. 394 *seq.*
Alexander, "Moral Order," pp. 34 *seq.*
Radestock, "Habit and Education."
Aristotle, "Nic. Eth.," Bk. II.

CHAPTER VII.

CLASSIFICATION OF MORAL EXCELLENCES.

Sidgwick, "Methods," Bk. III., ch. ii.
Muirhead, "Elements," pp. 175 *seq.*, 207 *seq.*
Alexander, "Moral Order," pp. 248 *seq.*
Stephen, "Science of Ethics," pp. 172 *seq.*
Whewell, "History of Moral Philosophy," additional lectures, Lect. ii.

On Prudence.

Sidgwick, "Methods," Bk. III., ch. iii.
Aristotle, "Nic. Eth.," Bk. VI.
Bentham, "Deontology," vol. ii., pp. 81 *seq.*

On Justice.

Sidgwick, "Methods," Bk. III., ch. v. and vi.
Grote, "Moral Ideals," pp. 262 *seq.*
Mill, "Utilitarianism," ch. v.
Aristotle, "Nic. Eth.," Bk. V.
Spencer, "Principles of Ethics," Part V.

On Courage.

Aristotle, "Nic. Eth.," Bk. III., vi.-ix.

Sidgwick, " Methods," Bk. III., ch. x., § 1.
Stephen, " Science of Ethics," pp. 175 *seq.*
Green, " Prolegomena," pp. 277 *seq.*

On Temperance.

Aristotle, " Nic. Eth.," Bk. III., x.-xii.
Sidgwick, " Methods," Bk. III., ch. ix.
Stephen, " Science of Ethics," pp. 190 *seq.*
Green, " Prolegomena," pp. 281 *seq.*

On Benevolence.

Sidgwick, " Methods," Bk. III., ch. iv.
Bentham, " Deontology," vol. ii., pp 189 *seq.*

On the Individual and Society.

Muirhead, " Elements," pp. 151 *seq.*
Alexander, "Moral Order," pp. 81 *seq.*, 112 *seq.*

CHAPTER VIII.

ETHICS IN RELATION TO THEOLOGY AND LAW.

Morality and Theology.

Gizycki and Coit, " Student's Manual," ch. viii.-ix.
Sidgwick, " Methods," pp. 500 *seq.*
Grote, " Moral Ideals," ch. xxi.
Marlensen, " Christian Ethics " (General).

Morality and Law.

> Grote, " Moral Ideals," ch. x.; Appendix.
> Fowler, " Principles of Morals," Part II., pp. 146-159.
> Sidgwick, " Methods," Bk. I., ch. ii.
> Bentham, " Principles of Legislation," Part I., ch. xii.
> Green, " Phil. Works," vol. ii., pp. 448 *seq.*

CHAPTER IX.

HISTORY OF ETHICS.

Besides Sidgwick's "History of Ethics," and the portions of Erdmann or Ueberweg which deal with the ethical theories of the different philosophers, the following will be found useful:—

A. *Greek and Latin.*

> Zeller, " Socrates and the Socratic Schools."
> „   " Plato."
> „   " Stoics, Epicureans, and Sceptics."
> Martineau, " Types of Ethical Theory," vol. i., pp. 23-111.
> Plato, " Protagoras," " Gorgias," " Philebus," " Republic."
> Aristotle, " Nicomachean Ethics."
> Wallace, " Philosophy of Aristotle."

B. *English.*

> Hobbes, " Leviathan," especially ch. viii.-xvi.

Locke, "Essay," Bk. I., iii.; Bk. II., xxviii.; Bk. III., xi., § 16-17; Bk. IV., iii., § 18; Bk. IV., § 7; Bk. IV., xii., § 8.

Shaftesbury, "Characteristics," especially "Inquiry concerning Virtue."

Clarke, "Boyle Lectures," 1704-1705.

Butler, "Sermons," especially I.-III., XI.; together with the "Dissertation upon Virtue."

Hutcheson, "Moral Philosophy."

Hume, "Inquiry concerning the Principles of Morals" (in the "Essays").

Adam Smith, "Moral Sentiments."

Price, "Chief Questions and Difficulties of Morals."

Reid, "Essays on the Active Powers."

Stewart, "Outlines of Moral Philosophy."

Paley, "Moral and Political Philosophy," especially Bks. I.-IV.

Bentham, "Principles of Morals and Legislation."

Bentham, "Deontology."

Mill, "Utilitarianism."

Martineau, "Types of Ethical Theory," vol. ii., pp. 394 to end.

c. *German.*

Caird, "Critical Philosophy of Kant," vol. ii., pp. 143-405.

Kant, " Critique of Practical Reason and Metaphysic of Morals," translated by Abbott.
Green, " Phil. Works," vol. ii., pp. 83 *seq.*
Schopenhauer, " The World as Will and Idea," *passim.*
Courtney, W. L., " Constructive Ethics," Bk. III.

APPENDIX B.

QUESTIONS FROM LONDON UNIVERSITY B.A. PASS PAPERS, 1883-1892.

1. ARGUE the question whether all Voluntary Action is for pleasure or from pain. (1883.)
2. Can a man act wrongly otherwise than through ignorance? (1883.)
3. Show what different lines were taken by English ethical thought in reaction from Hobbes. (1883.)
4. Enumerate the chief forms of Intuitional Morality exhibited by English thinkers. Explain the terms Moral Sense, Moral Sentiment, and Moral Reason. Why has the question of the origin of these forms of moral consciousness been regarded as of special ethical importance? State your own views on this point. (1884.)
5. Explain the following: Determinate and Indeterminate Duties; Cases of Necessity and Cases of Conscience; Natural Rights; Equity. (1884.)
6. Compare the Utilitarianism of Bentham and of J. S. Mill. State and examine the proof of the Utilitarian principle advanced by the latter. (1884.)
7. Distinguish the notions of Vice and Crime: and

determine exactly how far they overlap and why.

What corresponding distinction is there in regard to Virtue? (1885.)

8. When a man acts, is it what he desires, or what he designs, or what he effects, that is the proper subject of moral judgment?

Explain the distinction of *formal* and *material* rightness of actions; and consider how far it has a meaning for the Intuitionalist. (1885.)

9. How does Utilitarianism obviate (or seek to obviate) the objections that may be urged against Egoism as a Theory of Morals? (1885.)

10. Analyse the notion of Moral Responsibility, referring to the ultimate facts in human nature which seem to you to be involved. (1886.)

11. How has it been attempted to reconcile diversities of moral judgment in different ages or places with the Intuitional doctrine of the Moral Faculty? (1886.)

12. State briefly what you consider to be the strongest arguments in support of the position that the only end for action is pleasure, and discuss their value. (1886.)

13. Discuss the psychological basis, and inquire into the sufficiency, of Selfishness as a system of morality. (1887.)

14. What reason is there in calling the Moral Faculty a Sense?

Distinguish between Moral Instincts and Moral Intuitions; and consider what evidence there is for the existence of either. (1887.)
15. Are the Motive and the Intention of an act the same or different?

How far is an Intuitionist bound to regard, and a Utilitarian bound not to regard, the consequences of his action? (1887.)
16. Discuss the grounds on which it has been held that primitive impulses, whether Appetites, or Desires, or Affections, are disinterested in character. What significance has the decision of this question been held to possess for ethical theory? (1888.)
17. Examine the grounds advanced by Utilitarianism for the obligation on the individual agent to promote the general welfare. (1888.)
18. In what way do you consider the authority of the moral judgments assigned to Conscience would be affected if it could be shown that Conscience is a complex and developed fact of mind? (1888.)
19. Is it possible for the individual to do more than his duty? (1888.)
20. "The moral end is self-realization." "Morality consists in altruism." Compare these ideas. Is it possible to reconcile them? (1889.)
21. How far do duties arise out of social relationships? and how far are they purely individual? (1889.)
22. Virtue has been defined as the habit of choosing

the mean between extremes. Critically examine this definition. (1889.)

23. How far have ethical theories been affected by psychological doctrine? And how far has jurisprudence been affected by ethical theory? (1889.)

24. Indicate the points in the psychological analysis of Emotion and Action that seem of most significance for ethical theory. (1890.)

25. Comment on the distinctions that have been drawn (a) between what is *absolutely* and what is *relatively good*, and (b) between *natural good* and *moral good*. In the course of your answer consider the doctrine that pleasure and good are identical. (1890.)

26. In what relation does Utilitarianism place virtue to happiness? (1890.)

27. " The contrast between the morality which appeals to an external standard, and that which grounds itself on internal conviction, is the contrast of progressive morality against stationary, of reason and argument against the deification of mere opinion and habit." Consider this passage. (1890.)

28. On what grounds does Utilitarianism teach that the individual is bound to promote the general welfare? (1891.)

29. Are the Good and the Right identical? If not, what place do you assign to them respectively in a system of Ethics? (1891.)

30. Critically examine the statement, "All morality is social." (1891.)
31. Suppose it proved that the conscience has been evolved out of elements wholly unlike itself; would that discovery affect in any way its mature deliverances? (1891.)
32. Is desire always directed to the attainment of pleasure? Point out the ethical bearing of the question. (1892.)
33. By what method can we best determine the standard of right and wrong? Is it correctly described as induction from facts? (1892.)
34. How would you estimate the degree of moral goodness or virtue manifested in an action? (1892.)
35. Is all virtue reducible to regard for others? (1892.)

INDEX.

ÆSTHETIC view of Ethics, 124 seq.
Altruism, 76, 83.
Aristotle on summum bonum, 23; on φρόνιμος, 48; on habit, 160; his list of virtues, 166; on prudence, 174; on temperance, 176; on happiness, 26; on ethics as an art, 125.
Arithmetical hedonism, 75.
Art and morality, 124 seq., 128 seq.
Austin, 62, 153.

Bentham, 195; on sanctions, 54; on moral arithmetic, 68; on principle of distribution, 89.
Bonum, 22.
Butler, 87, 121 seq., 191.

Calculus, hedonistic, 59.
Cardinal virtues, 166.
Cases of conscience, 185 n.
Cases of necessity, 185 n.
Casuistry, 185.
Categorical imperative, 56.

Character, 3.
Clarke, 109, 189; his rule of equity, 84, 111; his rule of love or benevolence, 85, 111.
Classification of ethical theories, 16; of virtues and duties, 165.
Conduct, 1.
Conscience, 136 seq., 146, 147 seq.; origin of, 148.
Crime, 183.
Cudworth, 137, 189.
Cumberland, 189.
Cycle of ends, 39.

Deduction in ethics, 10.
Dependent ethics, 17, 88.
Desire, object of, 150.
Determinism, 156.
Dualism of the practical reason, 78, 113.
Duty and duties, 57; indeterminate duties, 62; duties to self, 169.

Egoism, 76, 86.
Emotion, moral, 144, 148.

Equity, 177.
Equity, Clarke's rule of, 84, 111.
Equilibrium of social order, 37.
Evolutionary ethics, 19 *seq.*, 95 *seq.*
Extra-regarding duties, 168.

Fame as an end, 24.
Formal rightness, 49.
Freedom of the will, 155.

God, 34, 122.
Good, 21 *seq.*; as relative, 43; cycle of goods, 38.
Greatest happiness principle, 79.
Green, T. H., 34, 122.
Grote, J., 27, 60.

Habit, 159.
Happiness, 25, 81.
Happiness and virtue, 82.
Hedonism, 17 *n.*, 28 *seq.*
Hedonistic calculus, 68 *seq.*
Hedonistic paradox, 151.
Highest want, 35.
Hobbes, 188.
Humanity as an end, 41 *seq.*
Hume, 138, 193.

Ideals, 118.
Imperatives, 56.
Imperfect rights, 51; obligations, 61.
Impulse, virtues of, 172.

Independent ethics, 17, 104.
Individual and society, 170.
Innate moral faculty, 117, 137.
Intention, 153.
Intuition, 11, 100; examples of ethical intuitions, 106, 111, 113 *seq.*
Intuitionism, 103 *seq.*; dogmatic, 105; empirical or perceptional, 10; philosophical, 109; objections to, 114.

Jural view of ethics, 38, 45 *seq.*
Jus naturale, 53.
Justice, 176 *seq.*

Kant, 114; on humanity as an end, 41; on rightness, 48; on categorical and hypothetical imperatives, 56; on obligation, 61; on freewill, 157.

Law, 43.
Law of nature, 43.
Locke, 109, 189.

Martineau, 105.
Material rightness, 48.
Merit, 64, 183.
Mill, J. S., 196; proof of hedonism, 29 *seq.*; proof of utilitarianism, 84; on quality of pleasure, 71; on justice, 197.

Morality and law, 181; and religion, 77, 179.
Motive, 153; mixed motives 154.
Natural rights, 51; natural law, 53; natural good, 22.
Nature, 44, 119 *seq*.

Obedience to law, 183.
Obligation, 53.

Paley, 25, 195.
Perceptional intuitionism, 10.
Perfection as an end, 33.
Perfectionism, 122.
Plato on pleasure, 28; on list of virtues, 166; on good, 23; holds vice involuntary, 161.
Pleasure, 28; unreal pleasure, 70; impure pleasures, 26; commensurability of pleasure, 70; quality of pleasure, 71; pleasure and desire, 150.
Predicate, ethical, 5.
Principle, virtues of, 172.
Progress, 15, 19.
Prudence, 173 *seq*.
Psychology and ethics, 133 *seq*.

Quasi-moral sentiment, 145.

Reason, 56, 121, 139; functions of reason in conduct, 142; practical reason, 142; dualism of practical reason, 78, 113.

Reid, 106 *seq*.
Relative ethics, 17.
Religion and ethics, 77, 179.
Responsibility, 65 *seq*.
Right, 46 *seq*.
Rights, 50; determinate and indeterminate, 51; natural rights, 50; rights of man, 53.
Rousseau, 53.

Sanctions, 54.
Savages, moral perception of, 116.
Scope of ethics, 13 *seq*.
Selfish, men not necessarily, 152.
Sense, moral, 137.
Shaftesbury, 137, 190.
Sidgwick, proof of hedonism, 31; of utilitarianism, 84; on freewill, 157; on justice, 176.
Sin, 180.
Smith, Adam, 194.
Society and individual, 169 *seq*.
Socrates, 5, 12, 161.
Spencer, Herbert, 20; on obligation, 61; on excessive altruism, 78.
Standard of right, 15 *seq*., 48 *seq*.
Stephen, Leslie, 20, 97.
Stoics, 52, 119.

Sully on freewill, 155; on motive and desire, 154.
Summum bonum, 22, 37.
Syllogism, the practical, 10.

Temperance, 175.
Theology and ethics, 42, 77, 179.
Theories, ethical, classified, 16 *seq.*
Truth as an end, 25.

Utilitarianism, 18, 79 *seq.*; objections to, 84 *seq.*, 88 *seq.*, 97; vagueness of, 92.

Vice, 183.
Virtues, 62; classifications of 165 *seq.*; cardinal virtues, 166; theological virtues, 168, 180.
Vitality as an end, 95.
Voluntary, wrong-doing how far, 161.

Wages, 177.
Wisdom as an end, 24.

www.ingramcontent.com/pod-product-compliance
Lightning Source LLC
Chambersburg PA
CBHW021828230426
43669CB00008B/906